GET
REAL

The ABCs of Authenticity

JOHN COTTON

GET REAL

The ABCs of Authenticity

TEN STEPS TO GENUINE LIVING

Get Real: The ABCs of Authenticity

© 2015 John Cotton
All rights reserved.

No part of this book may be reproduced or transmitted in any part by any means without the express written permission of the author.

The material in this book is for informational purposes only and is not intended to diagnose, treat, or cure any illness or condition. If you require medical attention, seek care from an appropriate licensed professional.

Canadian Cataloguing in Publication Data

ISBN: 978-0-9940796-0-2

Layout and Design by
words ... along the path
a branch of One Thousand Trees
www.onethousandtrees.com

Printed in Guelph, Ontario, Canada by
M & T Printing Group

The road to enlightenment is paved with authenticity, not imitation.

– Alan Cohen

Contents

Why Authenticity?	ix
Welcome	xi

Part I: Principles

Chapter 1: Embracing Experience	3
Chapter 2: The ABCs of Authenticity	21
Chapter 3: *A* is for Awareness	37
Chapter 4: *B* is for Being	55
Chapter 5: *C* is for Communication	77

Part II: Practices

Let's Experiment	105
Step 1: Notice	109
Step 2: Breathe	113
Step 3: Listen	117
Step 4: Recognize Emotions	131
Step 5: Examine Your Thoughts	141
Step 6: Feel Your Feelings	147
Step 7: Share Responsibly	153
Step 8: Make Distinctions	157
Step 9: Play with Options	167
Step 10: Create Yourself	175

Farewell	187
Acknowledgments	189
Bibliography	191
Index	195
About the Author	203

Why Authenticity?

Why

I believe in real relationships.

Life happens in relationships. Whether it's your relationship with yourself, with another, or with a higher power, the meaning and fulfillment you experience in life depends intimately, and ultimately, on relationships. Real relationships are vehicles of unlimited potential. Real relationships affirm our deepest values. Real relationships are relationships that work.

I believe you can create real relationships in your life.

Innate within you is a natural human capacity to transform your relationships into real relationships of deep connection and enjoyment. Real living starts when we get real, with ourselves and with each other. It means looking courageously at the truth of our lives, embracing the experiences it brings, and communicating our experience powerfully and congruently to others.

I believe you are powerful enough to handle all your experience.

Life comes with challenges, with sorrow and with pain, especially in relationships. Whatever you are facing now and however life is challenging you to grow, you are powerful enough to handle *all* of your experience. The human spirit is always greater than what is happening or has happened, and it can triumph over it. Your spirit has access to all the power you need to transform or transcend your experience.

I believe you have the answers you're seeking inside you.

I believe you have, as a spiritual being, an *authentic self* that is clear and purposeful about why you're here and what's really important. When you consciously handle your experience and get in touch with what's real—what's really true for you—you'll be empowered to find workable solutions to life's problems. I believe you can rediscover your authentic self and learn what matters most to you—what's *genuine*—and act on it with courage and conviction to create a life you love.

I believe you can live a genuine life.

How

Real relationships are built on principles of conscious living and sustained by practicing those principles in everyday life. Genuine living is a *principle-centered and practice-driven* means of creating flourishing relationships with God, Self, and Other.

Genuine living also respects the vital role your spiritual (non-material) nature plays in empowering your life, as well as the critical importance of effective communication in sharing who you are with the world. Hence, this way of creating real relationships is also *spiritually-oriented and communication-based*.

Finally, real relationships and genuine living are rooted in what we hold most dear. Through meaningful dialogue about what we value and purposeful action to embody it, we build true character and community.

What

Authenticity is a core component of genuine living. Being authentic connects us deeply with the human experience, which is the engine of all personal and spiritual growth. Just as knowledge of the alphabet is critical to understanding and creating language, knowing the ABCs of authenticity is essential to understanding your experience of life and recreating it anew.

*How would you describe
the taste of an orange?*

Welcome

I'm delighted that you're here. By now, you have a pretty good idea of what I believe and what I'm passionate about, but you might be wondering why I'm asking you about the taste of an orange. Let me explain.

First, though, I want to thank you. I appreciate your decision to invest your valuable time in understanding yourself and your relationships, and I'm honored by the trust you've shown me in opening this book as part of that journey. So, thank you for your time, your trust, and your commitment to your own growth.

I'm excited to share the ABCs of authenticity with you and I'm confident that—as you use them—they will help you discover your authentic self and create incredibly rewarding, real relationships in your life. Now, back to oranges: How *would* you describe the flavor of an orange to another? Is it possible to describe that experience to someone who hasn't tasted it already?

Here's my point: being authentic is an *experience*, not a theory, story, or explanation. Hence, this book is not merely "about" authenticity. That kind of book would just try to describe the flavor of an orange. This book is about three principles and ten practices that will help you create the experience of authenticity, giving you a new taste of life, a flavor of genuine living.

Fortunately, you've probably had at least some appetizers of authentic experience in your life already. We tend to recognize when someone is being real and authentic—it resonates with the authentic self in us. Often we see it in children. You might also have had moments where you stepped outside your usual limits and experienced yourself being genuine and fully expressed. Do you remember the last time that happened? Often, those experiences are like a breath of fresh air.

They're enlivening, invigorating, and memorable. At such times, we may suddenly feel fully alive.

In Part I of this book, we'll examine the ABCs of authenticity—awareness, being, and communication—and explore how those principles are tied up with your experience. In Part II, you'll learn ten simple but powerful practices based on the above principles that are enormously helpful in handling or creating experience, and you'll understand how each one relates to the ABCs of authenticity.

But don't take my word for it—everything I share comes from my experience. This is a book about my beliefs and what works for me. Put what you read to the test using your own experience. Try it out for yourself. Reading about the principles can be insightful and entertaining, but only by applying them in your daily living can you initiate the amazing transformation that is possible for you in the way you experience life *and* in the way others experience you. So I invite you to play with—*and practice*—these principles, and to discover for yourself their power to provide you a real taste of the fruits of genuine living.

If that sounds daunting, don't worry—nothing is required of you that you aren't already doing in your life. If you're like most people, you're probably already doing a lot. In following these steps, you don't have to do more. Instead, you'll uncover a new way of being that enhances and enriches your experience of life through whatever you're already doing or not doing.

I hope you will enjoy these experiments with experience and use them to help you discover...*you!*

With gratitude,

John Cotton

p.s. I also invite you to create your experience of reading this book. If you love tools and practical application, go ahead and skip straight to Part II and pick up a practice or two to implement right away. For example, you could incorporate any of the first three steps (noticing, breathing, and listening) into your experience of reading the rest of the book. Or, if you prefer to find out about the principles first, turn the page and dive right into Part I, which will touch on some of those practices anyway.

There's no right or wrong way to read this book, so choose your own adventure. Have fun with it!

Part I: Principles

*Principles are the territory. Values are maps.
When we value correct principles, we have
truth—a knowledge of things as they are.*

– Steven R. Covey, *The 7 Habits of Highly Effective People*

Part I: Principles

*Ultimately we have but one function —
to experience experience.*

– David R. Hawkins, *Power vs. Force*

Chapter 1: Embracing Experience

We do everything for the experience. That's the motivation behind all our endeavors—some kind of experience. Sometimes we simply want to understand our experience, but usually we want to change our experience.

For example, what motivated you to read this book? Why did you take your last trip? How come you play with your kids, or visit your friends? What drove your most recent purchase decision? Pause for a minute and consider your answers. What experience do you seek?

Generally, we want to experience happiness, joy, fulfillment, security, safety, belonging, confidence, enthusiasm, aliveness, peace, and love. I've never met anyone who tells me they want to experience as much unhappiness, suffering, pain, sorrow, anger, insecurity, and uncertainty as possible. Yet life comes with those experiences, too. And I have met many people, myself included, who invested enormous amounts of time and energy wanting more desirable experiences and chasing after them, only to find them elusive, and running away from difficult experiences, only to find them persistent.

M. Scott Peck wrote in the opening line of *The Road Less Traveled*, "Life is difficult." Sometimes life's difficult experiences occur in overwhelming intensity. They seem so big and powerful that we fear we can't handle them, that they will overwhelm and destroy us. This is especially true when we are young and vulnerable to the world. So we try to avoid and prevent these experiences, to control them and keep them hidden from ourselves and others. And we learn our lessons well. In fact, we lose ourselves in the attempt to control our lives and, thereby, our experience of life.

But this loss of authentic self is a terrible price to pay. Having contorted and hidden ourselves so as to avoid our experience of life, we are separated from life itself, which creates awful difficulties for being fully alive! It means we lose our capacity to consciously create our experience, we feel alienated from ourselves and each other, and we encounter endless obstacles to understanding our lives, to living compassionately with one another, to being human.

How can we rediscover ourselves and reclaim our lives? When we consciously embrace the fullness of our experience, when we *get real* with what's real, we begin to rediscover the truth of who we are and what's really important. When we share and communicate our experience of life powerfully with others, they *get us* and are liberated to discover who they are, too. In this process, paradoxically, the difficult experiences of life suddenly matter less, and those experiences we once sought so desperately suddenly begin to present themselves with surprising ease. We become connected to our authentic self, to life, and to each other.

Embracing experience is the key to finding yourself and living a genuine life. The good news is, your experience is absolutely free! The price of admission was paid for at birth, securing you a lifetime of human experience until your death. It's a nonstop experience extravaganza! Of course, if you're reading this book, chances are you're interested in a different way of dealing with all this seemingly unasked-for experience, and also of consciously creating the experiences that align with your deepest values and make life worth living.

Being authentic—*getting real*—is a process of inner discovery and self-realization that's deeply rooted in experience: your experience. The ABCs of authenticity—awareness, being, and communication—that you will learn about in the coming chapters are foundational principles for powerfully handling your past experience and passionately creating your future.

In this chapter, we'll begin that journey by asking some important questions about experience. What kind of experience do we want the most? What's the relationship between me and my past experience? Who am I, authentically? And what is needed in order to embrace experience and get real in relationships? To begin, let's look at the importance of connection and what I call the vulnerability problem.

Connection—It's What We Want

Connection is a vital part of living from your authentic self. When someone says, *"Get Real!"* they are inviting and challenging you to get connected with reality and to confront what's true about your experience. Of course, your reality or truth may differ from how they see it, but an honest exploration of such differences as we touch each other's worlds is an essential part of human connection.

This process of checking out reality together, by sharing openly and responsibly about our experiences, is an integral part of creating real relationships of deep connection. Life happens in relationships. Real relationships—with God, Self, and Other— are the context of human life. The quality of our connections in those relationships gives meaning and purpose to our lives.

In the foreword to the twentieth-anniversary edition of his best-selling book, *Getting The Love You Want*, Harville Hendrix, the founder of *Imago Therapy*, summarizes his life's work as being all about helping couples establish or restore connection. Connection, he says, is all of humanity's yearning, the experience we seek above all else. Of his many years of clinical practice he writes, "We have one diagnosis of unhappy couples—ruptured connection, and we have one goal in therapy: helping them restore awareness of connection with each other."

In short, we're hard-wired for connection. As a social species, this fundamental yearning shows up in all our relationships and evidence of its importance abounds in our lives.

Physically, we are utterly dependent at birth on connections with our parents or caregivers for many years, much longer than most mammals. We are born helpless, with an instinct for attachment, and needing social connections to help us grow and survive. Research studies have shown that babies deprived of physical connection and bonding with primary caregivers fail to grow and thrive, and physical touch remains an important health factor throughout our lives.

Mentally, we process information in terms of connections. Did you know the human brain is essentially a complex pattern-matching device that identifies meaningful connections in your experience? Built of trillions of neural pathways, some parts of the brain can and do change adaptively with learning and experience. Known as neuroplasticity, this process of remaking cellular connections literally alters how your brain works.

Socially, we seek connection with family, friends, colleagues, and other peer groups. The quality of our relationship connections in these groups greatly influences our success and satisfaction in life. In recent decades, innovations in technology have resulted in an explosion of new ways for us to connect and communicate, from cell phones to the internet. The proliferation of social media can be viewed as a great, global experiment celebrating human connection.

Spiritually, connection is a drive for wholeness, the end of separation (duality), and unity with the one spirit of all things in an interconnected universe. On our spiritual journeys, the rich landscape of human experience offers unlimited opportunities to evolve and grow in our relationships with God, Self, and Other. We could say that life is basically a grand adventure in connecting, and the choices we make in the face of connection and disconnection form the lessons of our lives.

Physically, mentally, emotionally, spiritually, socially: we *want* to be connected. Often, however, we don't experience deep, meaningful connection. We feel cut off and isolated, disconnected from our authentic self and unable to be in genuine relationship with others. If connection is so vitally important, why do we struggle so greatly to connect? Why is it so hard to *get real* in relationships?

Vulnerability—It's What We Got

You may not remember your birth, but the fact is your first experience in this world was one of utter, excruciating vulnerability and sudden disconnection.

Prior to your birth, you were insulated in your mother's womb, floating in warm amniotic fluid, connected via the umbilical cord, with all your needs met. There you stayed for about nine months, growing in the relative safety and shelter inside your mother. Suddenly, at birth, you emerged into new sensations of light, sound, temperature, the full weight of gravity, breathing for the first time, and having your umbilical connection severed. It was, as the saying goes, your welcome to the real world!

Without someone there to care for you, you would not have survived long. In addition to being physically vulnerable in your new environment for many years to come, you were also psychologically vulnerable for an extended period. You had neither the physical nor mental capacity to cope effectively in the world, you depended completely on others to care for you, and most importantly, you seemingly had no choice in the matter whatsoever.

Like it or not, you were born into an extended, enforced, and seemingly unasked-for period of excruciating vulnerability. During this vulnerable period in which you had little control over the world, survival was a tricky business. At first, you relied on instinctual responses to help get your needs met, whether crying or cooing. Later, you began to develop an awareness of how your responses could influence the world around you. Motivated by a natural curiosity, you began to experience and experiment, to learn by trial and error: How can I influence my environment? How can I grow in my ability to control my body and the world around me? How can I be less vulnerable and more in control?

So you went about giving yourself authentically to life, making connections between your self-expression and your experience. You discovered what worked, what didn't, and what helped you survive and stay connected to the people whom you felt you could not live without. But these survival lessons weren't always easy, and often they came at a cost to the full expression of your authentic self.

Surviving Vulnerability

Perhaps if you showed anger and were punished, you learned to disown your anger and hide it from others, or even from yourself. On the other hand, if throwing a temper tantrum always got you what you wanted, you learned that getting upset or angry is a useful tool for dominating others and meeting your needs. If you were repeatedly told to be quiet when you were loud perhaps you squelched your authentic enthusiasm and exuberance. If you were ridiculed for making mistakes maybe you developed strategies to never stand out or speak up so as to avoid looking dumb or feeling embarrassed. If the powerful people (adults) around you wielded their power in hurtful or irresponsible ways perhaps you concluded you must disown your authentic power in order to be a "nice" or "good" person.

There are endless combinations and variations to these kinds of adaptations, or survival strategies, based on individual personality and experience. Every child has a unique temperament and authentic personality—a psychic fingerprint—right from the start. Most mothers will tell you that each of their children felt different, even in the womb. Like most kids, you probably initially lived vulnerably and openly, expressing your unique temperament and authentic self, until you experienced the often painful lessons of rejection, correction, conformity, and punishment.

In your naturally vulnerable state, such experiences were incredibly impactful, whether the form of rejection or punishment was subtle or extreme. Perhaps it was merely your father raising his eyebrows and shaking his head anytime you displayed your sexuality. Or maybe it was your mother's "Tsk, tsk" and wagging finger anytime you made a mistake. At the other end of the spectrum are life's more traumatic experiences: abandonment, divorce, disability, neglect, abuse, and death.

In this tender phase of excruciating vulnerability punctuated by jarring emotional events, our experience sometimes seemed too much to handle. Exposed to feelings of almost overwhelming intensity, it was easy to conclude, "I am my experience," and to believe, "I must defend against my experience in order to protect myself." So we learned our survival lessons well, burning them into our unconscious mind so as never to forget them. Sometimes, we also buried the memory of the experience, keeping only the lesson.

Over the course of a few decades, maybe more, you adapted and adjusted to the world around you, refining your survival strategies and gradually losing touch with your authentic self. Sometimes you went to great lengths to look good, fit in, be right, maintain control, or avoid pain. (If you went to high school, you almost certainly know what I'm talking about!) You constructed a false self—a defensive façade—to hide those parts of your authentic self or your experience that you deemed dangerous or unacceptable.

Psychologists call this developed aspect of the false self a *persona*, from the Latin word for mask. As the famous Swiss psychologist Carl Jung described it, the persona is "a kind of mask, designed on the one hand to make a definite impression upon others, and, on the other, to conceal the true nature of the individual." Thus, we hold this mask up to the world to influence others and protect ourselves.

That's how the persona develops: we learn what works and we wear it, psychologically speaking. We establish a self-concept that we deem safe (invulnerable!) and acceptable to others, and we build our mask to match it. With a mask, we begin to feel less vulnerable and gain some degree of influence in our interactions with the world. We cover up, repress, and disown those parts of ourselves that are judged as bad or wrong, holding up a mask instead.

With one or more masks in hand, you were then ready to "get your act together." You augmented your external identity built around your masks by tailoring your behavior and appearance, turning yourself into a full-blown actor on the stage of life. We all act out such roles: the people pleaser, Mr. nice guy, the sports jock, damsel in distress, macho man, super mom, the busy executive, urban cowboy, laidback hippie, hard rocker, sensitive male, the spiritual person, rebel without a cause, sophisticated intellectual, miss-perfectly-happy-pants, and so on. Unconsciously, we cast ourselves in these roles to support our broadest survival strategies of avoiding pain, looking good, being right, fitting in, and controlling others.

On the surface of our lives, masks and roles constitute an approved self-concept, or identity, representing who we think we should be in order to decrease our vulnerability and stay connected in life. Through this false, fabricated self we seek to get the applause and approval of others—from our parents, our friends, our colleagues, our community, and even our God. Armored this way, our vulnerability no longer feels quite so excruciating. We feel we have found a way to survive. At last, we believe, we have solved the vulnerability problem that has plagued us since birth.

Over time, however, the unfortunate and inevitable downside of putting on an act or wearing a mask is disconnection and inauthentic living. Masks hide our authentic self. They separate us from our inner truth and distance us from other people. While they may indeed help us gain limited acceptance in certain social situations, they cannot produce the experience of deep and meaningful connection we desire because they prevent us from sharing ourselves vulnerably and authentically with others. Even if someone responds favorably to my mask, it's not a satisfying experience because at some level I know they're not actually responding to me, but to a façade. They're only relating to a fictional character of my own making.

Unfortunately, most of us established our self-concept on the limited wisdom and narrow experience of childhood and we continue to base our role-playing decisions today on conclusions we drew at age five, nine, or sixteen! So ingrained in us have these masks become that we rarely question their existence or revisit their making. In fact, we may even be completely unaware that we're holding up so many masks and holding down so much of our authentic self and experience.

Ultimately, we pay a terrible price to conquer the innate vulnerability life thrusts upon us and to escape the sometimes painful experiences that accompany it. Our efforts to diminish the vulnerability we don't want to live with only succeed at the cost of the authentic connections we can't live without. Psychologists Hal and Sidra Stone poignantly observe this basic human conundrum in their book, *Embracing Our Selves*, stating:

> *As we examine the basic interactive patterns that disrupt relationships, it is clear that the primary cause of these problems is our inability to deal with our vulnerability.*

The Vulnerability Problem

To recap quickly what we've covered so far: most of us see vulnerability as a real problem. Through our childhood and teen years, we learn that our inherent vulnerability is a bad thing, often leaving us threatened and exposed to painful experiences or sudden ruptures in our connections with God, Self, and Other.

Without loving care and guidance from our parents or other trusting authority figures to help us through such difficult experiences, we come to believe—based on very limited but emotionally compelling evidence—that our vulnerability results in dangerous and unpredictable disconnection. We conclude it must be eradicated and psychic defenses erected to give us greater control over the world and our experience in it. Thus, we armor ourselves against our vulnerability by creating a persona, a set of masks we wear and present to the world. We put on an act, playing a role we believe will help keep us safe.

Canadian physician and author Gabor Maté, M.D., describes this human tendency by noting that we have two major needs: attachment (i.e. connection) and authenticity (i.e. being who we are). He argues that, for instinctual reasons, whenever authenticity threatens attachment, attachment trumps authenticity. In other words, if vulnerably being ourselves jeopardizes our connections with others, we prefer to preserve those connections by giving up being who we are and putting on masks instead.

But our masks work too well. Having hidden our authentic self even from our own awareness, we lose the ability to connect meaningfully, spontaneously, and joyfully with others from the truth of who we are. Life loses some of its aliveness and childlike wonder as we cease to live authentically and share ourselves freely with the world. This inauthentic living then breeds a new kind of pain—the agony of disconnection. Although our vulnerability may have seemed unbearable, we come to realize that the pain of disconnection from God, Self, and Other now makes life truly intolerable.

At this point, people often feel stuck between a rock and a hard place. Perhaps you've been there yourself or are stuck there now. Personally, I've faced this impasse a number of times. On one hand is the primal fear of vulnerability based on the pain of the past, and on the other is the agonizing pain of disconnection occurring in the present. How can we escape this prison of pain? How can we restore our wholeness and create lasting connection and fulfillment in our lives?

Vulnerability Creates Connection

Sooner or later, life rather reliably provides the lessons we need to free ourselves from the past and get connected in the present. We may, if we are fortunate, seize such opportunities to undergo a shift of awareness. We may realize that we are actually free to choose how we handle our inherent vulnerability. We can continue to hide behind masks and put on an act, or we can relate authentically to others and to the entirety of our experience. In short, we can *get real* with ourselves and others. If we do, we may also realize that our long-standing judgment against vulnerability was mistaken. In fact, quite the opposite is true: vulnerability *creates* connection.

In a 2010 TEDx talk that rapidly went viral to become one of the most popular TED talks of all time, vulnerability researcher Brené Brown presented conclusions from her extensive research into "whole-hearted" people, highlighting the link between vulnerability and connection:

> *In order for connection to happen, we have to allow ourselves to be seen. Really seen. Vulnerability is not weakness. It is our most accurate measurement of courage. The whole-hearted [people whom I studied] had connection as a result of authenticity. They let go who they thought they should be in order to be who they were. They fully embraced vulnerability. What made them vulnerable made them beautiful.*

Living genuinely or whole-heartedly through authenticity means exposing ourselves as we really are. It requires dropping masks and defensive fronts to discover the truth inside of us. Yes, it's vulnerable. It feels risky and it takes courage. But it also opens a doorway to meaningful connection and to creating the experiences we truly desire.

I find this to be a great irony in our lives. We spend most of our early years mastering the world to protect us from our inherent vulnerability and learning to survive. Then we spend the rest of our lives mastering *ourselves* so we can decide once more to be vulnerable and finally thrive. We begin life in forced dependence, develop a measure of independence, and finally surrender to interdependence.

As our journey of self-realization unfolds, we discover that vulnerability isn't weakness after all. It's an important component of authenticity, catalyzing spiritual growth and paving the road to enlightenment. Vulnerability implies the courage to fully embrace our experience and share it honestly with others. As Brown explains, the word courage has its roots in the Latin word *cor*, meaning "heart", so having the courage to live authentically means "to tell the story of who you are with your whole heart."

Of course this sounds marvelous, but here's another authentic reality check: *authenticity ain't easy!* It requires courage, practice, and perseverance. Brown herself later described having had a three-day "vulnerability hangover" after her TED talk during which she didn't leave her house. Actually, few of us ever make it to being so vulnerable, let alone vulnerable on stage, never mind having a full-blown vulnerability hangover! We resist any experience of vulnerability before it even happens.

This is especially true of those experiences that don't fit with our approved self-concept or persona. Whatever experiences (e.g. getting angry, expressing sexual feelings, showing weakness, making mistakes, being powerful, and so on) that I determined early on were bad, wrong, or undesirable, don't fit with my idea of who I think I should be. Therefore, experiencing those experiences feels particularly dangerous and vulnerable because they threaten to make *me* bad, wrong, or undesirable.

If you recall, we became identified with our false selves, created our masks (persona), and adopted survival strategies in order to avoid being vulnerable to our experience in the first place. Authenticity, therefore, challenges us with the very thing we've spent most of our lives defending against—vulnerably experiencing *all* our experience, the totality of our authentic selves.

Can we fully embrace our experience? Can we rediscover our authentic selves? I believe we can. For me this challenge lies at the heart of real relationships, genuine living, and the process of self-realization. It is a vital part of any spiritual journey which asks the ultimate question of life: *Who am I?*

Authentic Identity

At this point, I want to explain what I mean by an authentic self, including some of the assumptions that are implied for me in that term. I also want to clarify how embracing experience is important not only for creating connection in real relationships but also for fueling spiritual growth.

As human beings, I believe we exist in two dimensions simultaneously: the world of humanity and the realm of spirit. The world of humanity is created by the perception of form whereas the realm of spirit is formless and eternal. As spiritual beings, we choose to enter a human form in order to learn and evolve through our experience. This popular quote from the French philosopher and Jesuit priest Pierre Teilhard de Chardin expresses it well:

We are not human beings having a spiritual experience: We are spiritual beings having a human experience.

In the world of humanity, we have many names for our true spiritual identity: Self, soul, consciousness, Light, immortal being, inner Christ, Ātman, divine spark, one life, etc. These concepts all point to the same basic truth that we are spiritual beings and that it is our spiritual nature that we strive to realize on a journey of self-realization or enlightenment.

At the same time, to be born human also means to inherit a legacy of limitation that shapes our experience. We inherit everything from animal instincts, a reptilian brain, genetic defects, unreliable memories, the circumstances of our birth, the decisions of prior generations, the collective unconscious, and more. We're fallible, imperfect, and mortal creatures, with widely varying abilities and capacities, strongly influenced by our evolutionary, animal heritage.

Being both animal (human) and angel (being) is part of the human condition. I feel any authentic identity requires at least acknowledging these aspects of who we currently are. The authentic self I've been referring to encompasses both—it is who you are in your human experience as well as who you are in spiritual essence. (When I want to refer to just your spiritual essence, I will capitalize the word Self.)

When you're in touch with your authentic self you have access to the totality of who you are. You aren't pretending to be enlightened nor are you denying your spiritual nature. You're connected to your humanity, with its inherent downsides, and also to the sublime qualities and unlimited potential of the human spirit. You're genuine about what's happening for you on all levels. You're deeply connected with what's true in your experience. You're related to what's real. In this way, your experience helps you to rediscover and express your essence.

Spiritual growth is a progressive awareness of truth, an increasing recognition of our reality, which we learn about through experience. When we fully embrace our experience and accept what's happening for us in our process of self-realization, then we're being authentic. By being authentic, we make the best use of our experience to grow as people and evolve as spiritual beings. The central importance of authenticity in any truth-seeking venture is eloquently expressed in these words from Alan Cohen, which I quoted in the opening pages of this book:

The road to enlightenment is paved with authenticity.

Striving to be authentic is as much a serious spiritual path as it is a practical means of creating real relationships. It is, however, a demanding practice. It confronts us with the vulnerability problem and with facing life's difficult experiences—those of deep disconnection. And this, as we've seen, is something we resist. Next, we'll look at how such disconnection only persists when we resist our experience.

Resisting Experience

As human beings, we spend most of our lives not knowing what we really want, but feeling darn sure, 'This ain't it!'

– Source unknown

At the beginning of this chapter I said we do everything for the experience, and that we're often motivated by a desire to change our experience. Frequently, we try to effect such change by resisting the experiences we're having—we hold up masks and hold down what's happening. We employ survival strategies to push away any unpleasant experience we *don't* want in the hopes that doing so will help us get to the experience we *do* want.

But it rarely works out that way. For some strange reason, the experiences we try most to avoid mysteriously keep happening. When they do, we tend to feel disconnected again from what we want, so we redouble our efforts at holding up our masks only to repeat the cycle over and over. We think we can get connected without being authentic, but it never works out that way, at least not for long.

Failing to fully embrace our experience and resisting it instead is the primary cause of our agonizing disconnection. To the same extent we have not experienced our experience, we are also cut off from our Self and thereby from each Other and from God. In this sense, the greatest block to experiencing what we really want lies in refusing to authentically handle the experience we already have.

As spiritual beings, we're here to *experience* experience. All our experiences can serve our spiritual journey if we handle them authentically, if we experience them consciously. Life always provides the experiences we need, the lessons we're here to learn in order to advance on our spiritual journey. If we refuse to *experience* our experience, if we resist or avoid it, then we deny an opportunity to learn and grow. Life, however, will not be denied: it will soon give us another opportunity via our experience.

Fortunately (or unfortunately, depending on your life view), anything unhealed in us—any experience we're not dealing with—will keep showing up in our lives until we're complete with it. This accounts for sayings such as *what you resist persists*, and *you can't stuff your stuff*. This is especially true in relationships. Any experience necessary for your spiritual growth will recur until you get real about it, deal with it, and triumph over it.

I've been humbled repeatedly in personal relationships where I've been presented with the same lesson time and again until I finally *got it*. In fact, even when I think I have *got it* a deeper variation of the same lesson will sometimes later appear. I've also learned repeatedly from my relationship with my body and health. I've experienced patterns of illness that have required me to get real with what was unhealed in me or incomplete in my experience. For many people, similar resistance shows up most clearly through patterns in their marriage or family relationships, or perhaps in their business or career. What patterns of recurring experiences have you noticed in your relationships?

Human history, including your personal history, is a great repository of experiences—some complete, some incomplete. The incomplete pieces are what we call unfinished business or emotional baggage, relics from the past that we carry around inside of us, perhaps even as cellular memory. This *unexperienced* experience is waiting for us to inquire into what it is trying to teach us. Until we do, it frequently blocks our ability to experience anything new.

We think power comes from resisting (escaping or denying) certain experiences and chasing after others. If we can control our experience, we believe, then we're powerful. But life doesn't work that way. Remember, we're *inherently* vulnerable. Real power—genuine empowerment—comes from embracing all our experience, choosing to connect with it vulnerably, and handling it authentically.

Embracing Experience

The ABCs of authenticity—awareness, being, and communication—will help you embrace your experience. As you become aware of your experience and are willing to be with it fully, you become able to communicate congruently what's happening for you in your relationships. You handle your life authentically. Similarly, as you become aware of what's really important to you, as you embody the innate qualities of your spiritual being that you value most deeply and communicate them to the world, you literally remake yourself and your experience of the world. You create a genuine life.

Embracing experience through genuine living, then, happens on two levels:

1. Handling experience
2. Creating experience

We typically get stuck handling our experience because of all the resistance we have to it, based on the vulnerability problem and the enormous investment we've made in all the false selves we discussed earlier in this chapter. We secretly believe that the way to create a new experience is by resisting any existing experience that's incompatible with our concept of self, rather than by handling it authentically.

This resistance makes it very hard to free ourselves to create a new experience. We just end up recreating the same experiences over and over until we acknowledge what's happening, learn from it, and restore our wholeness. Only then can we truly create something new. For that reason, much of this book will emphasize helping you handle your existing experience.

When you handle your experience and rediscover your authentic self, you'll also get connected with your higher Self, which knows the spiritual purpose of your human experience in life. Indeed, the innate qualities of the Self are the very source of all the experiences we genuinely want: love, joy, security, happiness, peace, courage, acceptance, and so on. As you surrender into this Self, you'll gain wisdom and clarity about your spiritual purpose and discover within you the capacity to *be* the experience you wish to create in the world.

Genuine living is a practice of living your life from your authentic self. From that place, you can humbly embrace *handling* your experience as part of your human inheritance, with all its many limitations and travails; and you can powerfully embrace *creating* your experience as part of your spiritual inheritance, with all the unlimited possibilities that entails.

In the next chapter, we'll look at the ABCs of authenticity in action and explore how they can support and serve you on this journey.

> *The privilege of a lifetime is to become who you truly are.*
>
> – Carl Jung

Chapter 2: The ABCs of Authenticity

In order to get real with our experience, three essential elements are required: *awareness*, *being*, and *communication*. These are the ABCs of authenticity, the basic building blocks of genuineness, and they will empower you to handle your experience and recreate it anew.

To help make these concepts concrete, let's take a look at the ABCs in action.

> ***Example 1:*** Imagine Jack, a middle-aged man, red-faced, stiff, nearly shouting:
>
> "No! Listen, I'm not upset! I'm just saying! Why can't you understand this simple point?!"
>
> Jack has little awareness of his own experience, and is resistant to being with it. He denies being angry, even when it's obvious to others what he's really feeling. Those around him are unlikely to hear the point he really wants to make because his inauthentic communication speaks so loudly.
>
> ***Example 2:*** Picture Susan, a professional woman, smiling and nodding, wearing a polite mask of agreement all while secretly thinking:
>
> "I'm so angry! What a ridiculous proposal! It will undermine everything we've worked for, and they don't realize it. But, of course, I can't say that."

Susan *is* aware of her feelings of anger, but she believes being angry isn't okay or that it isn't possible to communicate anger in constructive ways, so she doesn't share her outrage with the proposal. Instead, she communicates something entirely untrue for her. She's not being genuine.

Example 3: Visualize someone you love standing before you, looking you gently in the eye, taking a deep breath, and saying:

"When you yell at me, I feel hurt and scared inside. It's very important to me that we discuss this because I really want to make it work. To do that, I need us both to communicate with care and respect. Will you sit with me at the table so we can both feel heard?"

Your loved one is aware of their experience, they are willing to be with their feelings, and from within that vulnerable experience they are communicating the new experience they wish to create with you. They're being authentic and the effect is powerful. How would you respond?

These examples help illustrate that we're authentic to the extent that we bring all three of the ABCs to our experience. When these elements align, people get us—they see us as real and genuine. At such times, we're captivating, engaging, empowered, and powerful. As it turns out, authenticity is highly effective!

In this chapter, you'll gain a basic understanding of the ABCs of authenticity and how they work. Don't worry, you'll develop an in-depth understanding of these principles in the chapters that follow, and especially by doing the practices in Part II of this book. For now, the aim is to help you appreciate how these principles underlie every experience you have and why they're important to you in creating a new experience of living.

Baby Steps

To begin, let's consider a basic example of authenticity—a baby. Babies tend to command attention with their genuineness. They don't usually hide their experience or pretend it's something it's not. Take, for example, a hungry baby. In handling hunger, he will: (a) have some awareness of the experience of hunger, through sensations in the body; (b) be with that experience fully, like it or not, since in his vulnerability he cannot escape it; and (c) communicate about it congruently, possibly by rooting for a nipple or crying. He'll be real with his experience.

Now, I'm not glorifying babies here or suggesting you act like one. Babies remain limited in significant ways that constrain their experience and relationships. For example, they can't step back in awareness to look at their experience. They lack the capacity to consciously choose, through awareness, new ways of being that would alter their experience. Without language, their communication lacks concreteness and clarity and they cannot step out of their own experience to enter another person's world and understand *his* experience.

Still, babies teach us something valuable about handling experience authentically. They embody a very basic—we might say infantile—form of genuineness, but one to which we can profitably look for inspiration. Babies, despite limitations, command attention because they're congruent in how they handle their experience.

Part of the reason for this success is that babies are inherently vulnerable; they aren't hiding behind masks or putting on a show. As we have seen, though, this vulnerability isn't a choice and means that babies, as well as young children, are often faced with handling experience that is overwhelming in its intensity. As a result, they develop defense mechanisms to reduce their vulnerability exposure. Unfortunately, the cost of accumulating these layers of protection throughout childhood and adolescence is, quite commonly, loss of authenticity and connection in adult relationships.

Masking Imperfection: *Mr. Know It All*

One of my most vulnerable childhood experiences in the world of humanity was my mother's diagnosis with breast cancer. When I was just knee high to a grasshopper, my mother and I were playing together one Sunday in the local community pool. She was standing in the shallow end and repeatedly throwing a weighted diving ring into the deep part of the pool, where it would sink to the bottom before I would dive underwater to retrieve it. When I surfaced with the ring in-hand after my most recent attempt, I decided—instead of swimming over and handing it to my mother—to toss it back to her, accidentally striking her in the chest with it and bruising her.

Weeks later, when that bruise hadn't healed, my mother was diagnosed with breast cancer. Three years of chemotherapy, radiation, and hospitalization after that, she passed away. Too young and naïve to realize what her growing illness had meant, I was shocked. Thinking the usual self-centered thoughts that kids do, I reasoned that her death must have been my fault! I felt guilty, ashamed, sad, and afraid. And in the face of those painful feelings, I drew two very solid conclusions about my experience—*it's not okay to make mistakes*, and *people will die if I hurt or disappoint them*.

To compensate for my mistake and cover up my guilt and pain, I developed a mask of perfection to hide my secret imperfection. From here on, I would make no mistakes! The area where this survival strategy showed up for me most was in my studies. School, like life, is an opportunity to learn continuously by making mistakes. But for me, mistakes weren't safe to make—they had serious consequences! So I was unconsciously driven never to make a mistake or disappoint my teachers or my father. After all, if I were to make a mistake or disappoint them, they might die!

Thus, I wore a mask of perfection for years, striving at all costs to always know the answers. I developed a *Mr. Know It All* act that went along with my mask of perfection, which meant I needed to be right even if it meant making others wrong. I armored myself well against my vulnerability and fallibility and sought through these protective mechanisms to experience connection, approval, and safety, all while denying and repressing my feelings of disconnection, rejection, and insecurity. And that's pretty much how I started into adult life.

Now, I was going to ask you to imagine how well you think the above act, mask, and beliefs worked out in my early relationships but let's be honest, people: those relationships didn't work out! There's just not a lot of room for being *real* in a Mr. Know It All Broadway review where the lead actor can never admit he's made a mistake or was wrong. For that matter, there's also no room left for being human either.

It wasn't until I became chronically sick, deeply depressed, and disconnected from life that I found I could no longer deny the fact that my survival strategy wasn't working. I clearly did *not* know all the answers to healing my life or making my relationships work. It took a lot of pain and disconnection before I was willing to look within—to drop my mask and vulnerably embrace my experience. When I was finally willing to *get real* I was also able to *get living* and enjoy deep connection and fulfillment in relationships.

I now find great freedom in the words "I don't know." For me, they indicate courage and humility. I've come to appreciate in them a helpful beginning in pursuing life's most important questions. When I ask, "Who am I?" and don't try to supply the answer, I open myself up to what my experience is trying to teach me about both my human nature *and* my spiritual essence.

Some years ago, I also started looking forward to reconnecting with my mother in the realm of spirit. If I can impose an earthly experience on a heavenly realm, then I picture myself walking up to greet her as she, smiling mischievously, holds out a diving ring and lovingly asks, "Did you drop this?"

A-B-C, it's simple as 1-2-3!

In Chapter 1, we discussed two sides of the coin of experience, the currency of our lives. They were: (1) handling experience, and (2) creating experience. In this section, we'll examine how the ABCs apply to both kinds of experiencing as expressed in the following formula:

Awareness → Being → Communication

I want to remind you, however, that we also said authenticity ain't easy! If it were, we'd all be living more authentically or already be enlightened. Unlike the Jackson Five's famous song, the ABCs of authenticity aren't "easy as 1-2-3" but, as you can see from the examples so far in this chapter, they are simple enough to begin to understand and put into practice. Don't let this simplicity fool you, however. These simple principles are powerful. They simply work.

First, let's look at how the A→B→C process occurs in handling experience.

Handling Experience

Aware of my experience → Being with it fully → Communicating assertively

Authenticity begins in awareness. Whatever experience you are having, your power to handle that experience starts with the awareness of what's actually happening. This means being conscious. For example, a boxer or mixed martial artist will have a difficult time handling their experience in the ring if they're knocked unconscious or even temporarily stunned. The loss of awareness of what's happening in the fight means they're unable to handle their opponent, possibly stopping the match. Similarly, when sleeping you are less conscious of what's happening around you and your perceptions can be quite distorted. An alarm clock going off might occur in a dream as a ringing phone. As another example, your car might get stolen in the night, but you can't choose how to be with that reality until you wake up and become aware of it.

Spiritually speaking, unconsciousness means ignorance or unawareness. It implies sleepwalking through our daily lives, unaware of what's really happening in our experience, especially our inner experience of thoughts and feelings. Jack, the man in Example #1 at the start of this chapter, wasn't consciously aware of his anger experience and so couldn't deal with it authentically. We'll look further at awareness in Chapter 3.

In handling experience, *being* primarily means *being with*. It is the willingness to accept whatever we become aware of in our experience and to be with it, to own it, even when that's uncomfortable or painful. The art of *being with what is* involves the spiritual practices of non-resistance, non-attachment, and non-judgment of experience. By not arguing with the reality of our experience, not clinging or reacting to it, and not judging it as wrong, we create a sacred space in which to be with that experience and check it out. In that space, the experience already begins to transform; and from that space, we can be proactive and conscious in selecting a response. In Chapter 4, we'll look further at specific mechanisms people typically use to avoid being with experience, and I'll offer you some of my favorite strategies for maintaining a conscious connection to your experience.

Having become aware of your experience and allowed yourself to be with it, you can then choose to communicate that experience to others, or not. Sometimes just being with an experience changes it and you'll find there's no need to express what was only a passing form in awareness. At other times, being authentic requires you to communicate courageously the experience you're having. In Chapter 5, we'll look at how to create clear, effective communication through assertiveness and personal responsibility.

Next, let's walk through this A→B→C sequence again in the context of creating a new experience.

Creating Experience

Aware of what I value in my Self → Being those qualities →
Communicating my Self powerfully

When connected with your authentic self, you create your life through the awareness of what's really important to you. This means being conscious of what experiences you truly value. As we explored in Chapter 1, we tend to value connected experiences in which we feel joyful, happy, secure, courageous, peaceful, relaxed, confident, and so on. Such experiences are created by letting go of our false self and connecting with the intrinsic qualities of our spiritual nature, our true Self. In the process of self-realization, we evolve in consciousness as we realize these qualities of the Self and bring them into our experience.

When we're aware of what we value in our Self, we're able to consciously choose to bring it into the world. As we become conscious of who we want to be, we elect—through our own free will—to align with those qualities in our Self. We choose ways of being that bring those qualities to life in us. To create a new experience, we must, as Gandhi said, be the change we want to see in the world. Thus, the word *being* in this context means primarily a *quality of being* that we consciously choose to take ownership of, an attitude that we adopt, based on an awareness of what we value.

Finally, we decide how to best embody that quality of being by communicating it powerfully from a place of deep connection with our Self. Or, more accurately, that quality expresses itself spontaneously through us when we align with it fully. This means that our chosen way of being in the world determines our actions in it. What we do and have in life arise naturally from this powerful connection to the qualities we choose to be.

Authenticity: A Work in Progress

At this point, we have a more complete picture of authenticity than what we saw with babies. Genuineness requires that we strive to use, to the fullest extent possible, our natural human gifts of consciousness, self-awareness, free will, language, and self-expression, in order to manifest ourselves congruently in our relationships.

Developing these gifts, however, is a work in progress so it's important to realize that being authentic is as well. Authenticity isn't something we're likely to get right once and solve forever. Rather, it is something we will practice continually because we're continuously handling and creating new experiences in life.

When I speak of being authentic, I'm not suggesting we can ever be perfectly authentic. As my own experience attests, any attempt to appear perfect by manufacturing an identity from false masks is totally inauthentic! We can only be real to the best of our ability in any given moment, based on what we have access to through our limited and fallible human faculties. Therefore, in *getting real* and recovering from our false ways of relating, we strive—as one slogan in the 12-step recovery movement says—for *progress not perfection*.

This only makes sense, since perfect awareness isn't something we can achieve short of perfect enlightenment and authenticity *isn't* enlightenment, though it paves the way to it. For example, much of our experience is happening in our subconscious minds, where it's unavailable until we evolve further in awareness. In a similar vein, without some kind of enlightenment experience to arrest the endless activity of the mind, *so much* experience is happening for us at any given moment that it would be impossible for us to be with all of it fully all of the time. Nor could we possibly, even if we wanted to, communicate every thought or feeling we experience in our busy minds.

Hence, being authentic doesn't mean being perfect, scrupulous, or overzealous. It simply means handling the dominant elements of our experience to the best of our ability. Hence, babies tend to be authentic, making the best of their limited abilities. As adults, the more we become aware of what's happening inside of us, the more we can be with it and accept it, and the more we can communicate it accurately and concretely, the higher our degree of authenticity. So long as I'm honest about what I'm experiencing, other people will recognize and appreciate that it's authentic (real) for me, even if they have a different perspective or experience.

So give up any notion of perfection in your A→B→C of awareness, being, and communication. All that's required is to align these three elements with your experience to the best of your ability. When we are congruent this way with our experience, then we are empowered and powerful. We naturally command attention and inspire others.

Helping Relationships

This *congruence* of having all three ABCs aligned with our experience not only serves us well on our own spiritual journey, but it's also the distinguishing characteristic of any effective helping relationship.

Carl Rogers, the influential twentieth-century psychologist and founder of the humanistic psychology movement, spoke of helping relationships in very broad terms, being for him "any relationship where one or both parties intend to promote the growth, development, maturity, improved functioning, [and] improved coping with life of the other." In other words, a helping relationship helps the individual(s) change for the better, making greater use of their inner resources and actualizing their potential.

As such, any relationship in which we want to help the other person(s) grow and evolve is a helping relationship. From a spiritually-committed perspective, all human relationships in which we engage are potentially helping relationships, if that is our intention. If we wish to be of service in this way in all our relationships—as spouses, parents, friends, colleagues, community leaders, elected officials, employers, or therapists—then what can we bring to our relationships to serve our helping purpose?

In his classic book, *On Becoming A Person,* Rogers relates in everyday terms the foremost condition that empirical evidence identified as necessary for promoting growth in psychotherapy:

> *It has been found that personal change is facilitated when the therapist is what he is, when in the relationship with his client*

> he is genuine and without 'front' or façade, openly being the feelings and attitudes which at the moment are flowing in him. We have coined the term 'congruence' to try to describe this condition. By this we mean that the feelings the therapist is experiencing are available to him, available to his **awareness**, and he is able to live these feelings, **be** them, and able to **communicate** them if appropriate. [Bold emphasis mine.]

Being truly helpful to those around us, therefore, comes out of this congruence, the condition of matching all three ABCs of authenticity (awareness, being, and communication) with our actual experience. Incongruence, by contrast, is a state in which feelings are unrecognized, unowned, or unexpressed.

Of course, Rogers goes on to combine this foremost condition of a helping relationship with others, including unconditional positive regard and empathic understanding of the other person. However, without being *real* first, these other gifts are diminished. If I'm feeling annoyed or bored with another, but I'm not aware of that experience and not owning it, then my attempts to show understanding and communicate positive regard will be tainted by my incongruence.

Therefore, being authentic is potentially the greatest gift we can give, not only to ourselves but also to others. It may be surprising to discover that embracing our own experience is the best way to help other people. In the next section, we'll look at specific questions which can help further such service to the world by guiding us in the practice of authenticity.

Inquiring Into Experience

In both handling and creating experience, moving through the progression of A→B→C can be facilitated by simply asking certain questions. Questions direct our attention and help us uncover the truth. As we inquire into what's happening for us and question what we truly value, we become effective at embracing experience and living authentically. Here are some sample questions that can help you *get real* with your experience:

Handling Experience

    A. What's my experience now? What am I aware of? What do I notice is happening?
    B. Could I be with this experience without wanting to change it? Could I allow it to be?
    C. Do I need to communicate this experience? If so, how? What do I need to do or say?

Creating Experience

    A. What's my experience now? What's missing here that I value? What do I really want?
    B. Could I choose to bring what I value to this experience? Could I be that quality?
    C. How could I embody that quality? What do I need to do or say (or not do or say) to express it?

Often, just reading these questions is enough to raise your awareness and help you handle your experience more authentically or empower you to create what you genuinely desire.

In Part II of this book, you'll learn ten simple practices that will help you deepen your answers to these questions and move you forward on the path of authentic living. Those practices will put the principles of awareness, being, and communication into action in your life. As you'll discover by doing them, they can be tremendously helpful in cultivating real relationships and living a genuine life. (In fact, if you want to skip ahead and read the first one or two practices, they will also help you as you read this book!)

Interconnected ABCs

So far, I've presented the ABCs of authenticity as a linear process of A→B→C to make them easy to understand, but this isn't the only way they operate. These three elements are interconnected and operate simultaneously. Thus, a shift in any one of them can significantly influence the others, too.

In the coaching work I do with individuals and couples, I often focus on specific communication practices with my clients. You might recall that in the opening pages of this book, I described my approach to genuine living as "spiritually-oriented and communication-based." Often, communication provides an insightful and revealing window into the invisible realm of spirit. Communication, unlike awareness or being, occurs primarily in the observable world. It's rooted in language, including body language (what we see) and the spoken word (what we hear). Language reflects our awareness and qualities of being. As such, it makes for a very accessible entry-point to embracing experience. Often, simple changes in communication produce incredible results!

For example, I frequently assist clients to communicate in ways that help them get clear and concrete about their experience in terms of specific feelings, thoughts, and behaviors. These practices (some of which you'll learn about in Chapter 5 and try out in Part II) help develop a client's capacity to express himself precisely and directly, having an immediate impact on his self-awareness—that is, on what he must be conscious of in order to express his experience. The structure of these communication processes also supports the client to be with his experience as he communicates it, bypassing habitual resistance mechanisms that would normally cut him off from vital aspects of his authentic self. (We'll look more at those resistance mechanisms in Chapter 5). This brings about authentic self-expression in a manner that might better be described as C→A→B, or C→B→A.

Thus, through small changes in how clients communicate, big things happen in awareness and being: suddenly they become aware of an astonishing number of things they couldn't see before and they discover they can be with people, including themselves, in richly rewarding ways. This, in turn, opens up whole new possibilities for being and behaving differently. Needless to say, these are life-changing events in terms of the client's experience, especially in relationships.

Other combinations of the ABCs are equally valid. A sudden shift in awareness, or jump in consciousness, as we have seen, can dramatically alter how someone will choose to be in their life and how they will communicate. For other people, simply learning to be with whatever is happening, perhaps by breathing deeply and noticing sensations in the body, begins to raise their awareness and naturally influences how they express themselves (i.e. B→A→C).

Aligning the ABCs with our experience is the basis of authenticity and it can unfold in any sequence. Earnestly applying any one of the principles to our experience can quickly bring the others into play as well. Ultimately, *any* of the ABCs is a valid starting point for embracing experience and you can get started being authentic by handling any experience that's significant for you, even something from your past.

The Power to Choose

Until now, you may have believed you are simply a product of your past, that your experiences have made you the way you are. Perhaps you felt you had no choice regarding your past experience when you were so vulnerable. Maybe you believed you were, or still are, the victim of what happened to you.

Now, however, you can make a different choice. Vulnerability is not victimhood. While it may be true that you *had* limited options for coping with your experience in the past, especially as a child, now you have the ability to handle it using the ABCs of authenticity.

Today, you can revisit the past and become aware of what really happened—you can separate external events from your inner interpretations and conclusions about them. You can safely learn to be with whatever feelings you locked away and weren't ready to face on your own at the time. And, if necessary, you can communicate about your experience, for the sake of coming to know yourself, getting complete with someone in your past, or connecting with others who have faced similar challenges.

As you discover some of the masks you've been wearing to protect yourself, you'll be able to decide if these masks are still serving you today. What price has been paid for putting on these fabricated faces? What has it cost you? Clearly your masks served an important purpose at some point, but do they still? Often they do not.

At the same time, noticing our masks doesn't mean we will never wear them again. It simply means we're reclaiming the power to choose if we will do so. If someone asks me in passing how I'm doing when I'm having a rough day, I may consciously choose to say, "Fine, thanks," to avoid getting into a lengthy conversation or vulnerably exposing myself in a place I don't feel safe. But this is very different from believing I *must* be fine and behave that way, that I have no choice but to put on a happy face.

The power of conscious living lies so much in this power to choose our experience of life. Often, once we get a taste of authentic living, we decide our masks don't serve us very well and that choosing to be authentic serves us better. Old habits may die hard, but with practice we can learn to step out of the past, to put down our masks, and engage in genuine living.

Review

In this chapter, you learned that you are empowered and powerful in your experience to the extent that you bring all three elements of authenticity (awareness, being, and communication) to your experience. People who do this are captivating, influential, and alive.

We also revisited embracing experience, with its two parts: handling and creating experience. We denoted the process of aligning the ABCs with your experience as A→B→C, although it can happen in any order. This shorthand notation implies: (A) becoming aware of what's real and true for you; (B) being with the experience that you're aware of, or deciding from that awareness who you choose to be; and (C) communicating assertively and powerfully about your experience or your Self.

You also learned how authenticity is a critical factor in any helping relationship, discovered why it is always a work in progress, asked some key questions to help you inquire into your experience, and began stepping out of your past by realizing you can reclaim your power to choose. Being vulnerable and authentic is a choice that's available to you.

Now that you have a basic understanding of the ABCs and some appreciation of their importance, we'll dive deeper into each of them in the next three chapters.

*What is necessary to change a person is
to change his awareness of himself.*

– Abraham Maslow

Chapter 3: *A* is for Awareness

Awareness is the basis of consciousness. As spiritual beings, I believe we naturally seek to expand our consciousness, realize our potential, and evolve in our awareness of the truth. But what is true?

As we experience different levels of consciousness on our spiritual journey, what seems true or real changes quite dramatically. This difference is obvious between sleeping and waking states of consciousness (i.e. a dream no longer seems real upon waking), but even in our waking lives there are many different states of consciousness from which we perceive and experience the world.

For example, to someone whose state of consciousness is rooted in materially-based identifications (e.g. "I am my body"), the world might appear as a hostile, competitive, and dangerous place where survival of the fittest through the acquisition of power and material means is the name of the game. Life is very serious. To someone identified more with their spiritual nature, who wears the world loosely like a garment, it may seem a pleasant, rewarding, and cooperative place where people strive together to improve and enjoy their lives. Life is a shared adventure. To an enlightened guru who is free of the duality of perception and totally identified with the realm of spirit, the world of humanity might appear merely as an illusory place of our own making. Life is just another form of dream (the dream of form) we are dreaming until we awaken to the truth.

To illustrate the profound effect of consciousness on our lens of perception (and thereby on our experience of life), imagine your state of consciousness is like a tinted pair of glasses that you don't realize you're wearing. Unbeknownst to you, they color the way you see the world. If I'm in the blue state of consciousness, then to me the whole world takes on a blue hue. If you're in the pink state of consciousness, everything probably seems rosy. If blue represents sorrow/grief and pink stands for optimism/joy, our views of life will be very different!

Much more than just a passing mood, our state of consciousness sponsors our prevailing attitudes, worldviews, sense of identity, and conceptions of God and the universe. Everything we experience is colored by consciousness. What's true for any one of us, therefore, depends on our subjective experience as colored by our state of consciousness and reinforced through experience by conditioning. In *The 7 Habits of Highly Effective People*, Stephen R. Covey writes:

> *Each of us thinks we see things as they are, that we are objective. But this is not the case. We see the world, not as it is, but as we are—or, as we are conditioned to see it. When we open our mouths to describe what we see, we in effect describe ourselves, our perceptions, our paradigms.*

In other words, as we peer out through our lens of perception, we see things according to our prevailing paradigm of consciousness. The stratification of awareness into different levels of consciousness (blue, pink, green, etc.), each underpinning very different paradigms and worldviews, is what accounts for so much diversity—and disagreement—in the human experience.

To make this point abundantly clear, just think of all the conflict and differences of opinion you've experienced in your personal relationships! We literally see things differently through our unique lenses of perception, even when observing the same external events. Although there are many factors that influence perception, our state of consciousness dominates.

In this chapter, we'll explore the nature of human consciousness which so greatly influences our lives and I'll introduce you to three paradigms that can help you make sense of your experience and empower you to change it. We'll also have a brief look at the importance of mindfulness and observing the mind to increase consciousness. Finally, we'll take a peek at some of the complex energy patterns of consciousness that we often experience as the various talking voices in our heads.

Levels of Consciousness

Let's continue with our metaphor about different levels of consciousness that color our experience. Just as white light can be dispersed through a prism and the different wavelengths observed as colors of the visible spectrum, so can the light of consciousness (pure awareness) be dispersed into multiple bands, or energy levels, and experienced as different states of human consciousness, from the most horrific to the sublime.

On our spiritual journey of self-realization, the choices we make lead us to experience these different energy fields, each with their relative truths and apparent realities. As we encounter these different states of consciousness, we choose once more how to respond to what happens in our experience. Through free will, we can ascend or descend the levels of consciousness, leading to a subjective experience of heaven or hell.

Although the notion of *consciousness* was at one time pretty rare, it has become increasingly important in our social dialogue. We often hear talk now in the media of being more socially conscious, environmentally conscious, and spiritually conscious, reflecting a shift in our collective awareness. Similarly the terms personal growth, self-development, and spiritual enlightenment have become increasingly common. As we grow in awareness, whether individually or collectively, we find ourselves making different choices. Historically, we've seen mankind's overall consciousness evolve significantly, as expressed through more enlightened forms of government, civil and human rights, women's suffrage, environmental protection, and so on.

Fortunately, we humans have been involved in this business of evolving in consciousness for long enough now that we've amassed quite a collection of explanations and descriptions about the nature of consciousness and its different levels. The last half of the twentieth century, in particular, saw a global collaboration among scholars, philosophers, religious teachers, and spiritual leaders that helped sketch out the invisible spectrum of human consciousness for us to better see and understand. There have also been very fruitful efforts to integrate and synthesize the understanding of consciousness contained in all major wisdom traditions.

While many of these descriptions of the levels of human consciousness can be illuminating and life-altering, they can also seem quite complex and challenging to assimilate if this is your first introduction to such ideas. So for now, let's get real about consciousness and talk about it in simple terms that we can all understand and relate to in our lives.

Things and Experiences

In my coaching and training work, I sometimes ask clients to create a list of tangible things they want. This might include more money, a new relationship, a different job, a tropical vacation, a fast car, and a big house. If you want to play along with this exercise, go ahead and make your list of desired things now.

Next, we inquire into why they want these things. What will they experience once they have acquired those things? Often the answers include happiness, freedom, joy, intimacy, aliveness, peace, fulfillment, relaxation, confidence, and security. Again, take a minute to jot down your own answers.

Finally, I ask clients to compare the list of tangible *things* with the list of intangible *experiences* by asking a few questions. Do they, for example, know of anyone with a large house, fast car, or lots of money who doesn't experience much happiness, relaxation, or fulfillment? Yes, they do. Do they also know of people who experience a great deal of joy, freedom, and peace without possessing the things on the other list? Again, they do. The conclusion is that there's no intrinsic link between *things* and *experiences*.

With this (sometimes shocking) awareness, clients are then able to re-evaluate whether their current goals will really create the experiential results they want in their lives, and they can explore alternative (and sometimes much more direct) ways to create those experiences independent of things. This isn't to say material objects aren't valuable—conscious, happy people often enjoy possessing nice things—but on their own they don't have the power to make us happy. After completing this exercise, clients will often still choose to pursue many of the same tangible, material goals, but now the meaning and significance of those goals is altered by the shift in awareness they've undergone. Suddenly, they can approach their life aspirations from a different consciousness.

Be-Do-Have

The previous exercise offers us a glimpse of two very broad bands of consciousness: *being* and *having*. Between these is another wide band of consciousness centered on *doing*. In this section, we'll examine three paradigms of consciousness using these broad concepts of being, doing, and having. Exploring consciousness this way is very simple and it matches how we naturally tend to think about life in terms of what we want to be, do, and have.

Have-Do-Be

As we saw from the "Things and Experiences" exercise above, the consciousness of *having* frequently dominates our lives. So much of our consumer-based society is built around material things we want to *have*, which then determines what we *do*, so that we can someday *be* a certain way. This paradigm of consciousness promises, for example, "If I **have** the right things (more money, better job, bigger house, newer phone, etc.), then I can **do** what I want to do (go shopping, take a vacation, download that app) in order to **be** a certain way (happy, fulfilled, secure, at peace, etc.)."

Let's call this paradigm that emphasizes having, the Have-Do-Be paradigm. In this consciousness, we're primarily aware of what we'd like to possess, as a key part of who we think we are. Our identity is predominantly materially-based and our activities focus mainly on *getting* whatever we feel is important. This is quite common in the animal kingdom where so much activity is based on getting things like food, mates, territory, and so on.

One downside of this paradigm, however, is that we can never *have* enough to reliably *be* in a state of happiness, joy, love, security, or peace. There is also a sense of disempowerment and victimhood that accompanies needing to *have* before one can *do* or *be* because acquisition must come from outside ourselves. This level gives away personal power and is often characterized by a lack of energy, a heaviness and a strain to life. It only rarely produces, and certainly never sustains, the states of being which most of us are really seeking.

Do-Have-Be

The next paradigm of consciousness emphasizes *doing*. The promise of the Do-Have-Be paradigm is, for example, "If I can **do** well at this job, then I'll **have** more success and money, and I'll finally **be** happy." This consciousness drives so much activity, productivity, industry, and achievement in our modern world. We can see its prevalence in the everyday greeting, "How are you *doing*?" and in the inevitable cocktail-party question, "So, what do you *do*?"

There is more energy in this paradigm because, most of the time, we have the freedom and ability to choose what we want to do. We're more empowered and in charge of what we create in this state of consciousness, and our personal productivity and level of activity form a major part of our identity and self-worth.

Unfortunately, though, we can never *do* enough to *be* truly happy and fulfilled. We never quite measure up in the world, no matter how much we accomplish. We get stuck running on a treadmill of frenetic activity trying to do more, in order to have more, so that we can finally be at peace. But it rarely works. Completing a "to do" list might be the primary goal of a human *doing*—but we are human *beings*.

Be-Do-Have

In a consciousness centered on *being*, we consciously choose qualities of being that we value and wish to experience. For example, this consciousness might say, "I choose to **be** a happy and helpful person, so I will naturally **do** whatever expresses those qualities to myself and others, and I will **have** whatever happy and helpful people have, such as rewarding relationships and an abundance of opportunities to be of service."

In this paradigm, doing and having flow out of being. There's nothing I need to do or have in order to experience being peaceful, balanced, strong, courageous, etc., because those qualities are an innate part of who I am. They are intrinsic aspects of my spiritual nature, my true Self. They've only been covered up by aspects of my material nature.

There is enormous power and freedom in the Be-Do-Have paradigm because it isn't limited by external actions or possessions. No longer are we dependent on *doing* or *having* to create a state of *being*. This consciousness is reflected in Gandhi's encouragement to "be the change you want to see in the world."

You might also recognize this paradigm in the ABCs of authenticity because it underpins the A→B→C process of *creating experience* you learned about in Chapters 1 and 2. That process requires an awareness of the qualities of being that we value, a decision to be those qualities, and an ability to communicate whatever best expresses who we've chosen to be.

॰

In exploring these different paradigms of consciousness, I believe it's important to point out that there's nothing inherently bad or wrong about any of them. Each paradigm provides unique lessons and opportunities to grow, contributing to the possible range of human experience available to us as spiritual beings. Once we are aware of the different options, however, we can exercise our power to choose, selecting a paradigm that best supports the life we want to live.

Keep in mind, too, that these broad bands aren't distinct. Just as blue doesn't instantly become pink on the electromagnetic spectrum, the transition in consciousness from predominantly *having* to predominantly *doing* doesn't occur at a sudden point either, but spans a wide segment of the spectrum. Similarly, in choosing a paradigm that emphasizes *being* we don't suddenly stop *doing* or *having*, but the things we have and activities we do are freshly colored with new meaning. In any paradigm of human consciousness all three elements are present (being, doing, and having); what varies is simply the prevalence and importance of each one.

Language Reflects Consciousness

In the previous chapter, I shared that I often focus on communication habits with my clients because what we say reflects who we are. Said another way, our words reveal our worlds. This principle that language reflects consciousness is useful because it means that we can observe our use of language to become aware of our state of consciousness. To see how this works, let's look at an exaggerated example using a hot topic: sex.

Read the following three paraphrased statements about sex and relationships that I've heard men make, then decide for each one if it primarily represents a consciousness of *being, doing,* or *having*.

1. "Man, I'd sure like to get some of that! I've got to have her. Do you think we'll hook up with them at the party so I can get her number?"

2. "So…did you guys do it yet?" • "Hey, that's none of your business—and yes we did!" • "So…is she good

in bed?" • "She's great! We did it three times Saturday night!"

3. "I love being with her. It doesn't matter what we do, I just enjoy her company. When we connect sexually, it's such a loving, fun, and playful space for us to be."

These statements provide little windows into the inner worlds—the states of consciousness—of the speakers. In the first example, the possessive tone emphasizes *having* through getting. Sex is a conquest and an acquisition, an experience to be obtained for pleasure and used as an identity enhancer. The urge for sex may be experienced as a compulsive, uncontrollable desire and one can never get enough.

In the second exchange, the emphasis is on *doing* and the meaning of sex is based in performance, in successfully accomplishing the physical act. The focus on how one is doing it (how often, how well, what positions) drives the experience, possibly turning it into a sort of vigorous sexual Olympics that determines one's self-identity and value as a lover.

In the final example, the core of the experience is rooted in *being*—being together, being in each other's company or arms, and being expressive with one another. In fact, sex becomes secondary to this way of being together because it is only one of many possible outcomes that could unfold naturally from a place of deep, vulnerable connection between two human beings.

Through language, consciousness is revealed. At first, it's often easier to observe the prevailing state of consciousness in someone else's language rather than our own but if we listen carefully to what we say we can soon learn to identify the state of consciousness that sponsors our words. Interestingly, though, the vast majority of our words are never spoken aloud. Most of our communication is silently self-directed. Thus it can be helpful to turn within and notice what kind of language we use when speaking to ourselves.

A Voice in the Head

Have you ever noticed there's a voice in your head that never stops speaking? If you just heard yourself say, "What voice? What's he talking about? There's no voice in MY head!" — well, my friend, *that's* the voice! Now, perhaps your voice was more subtle, saying instead, "Oh I know that already." Or maybe it thought, "What a ridiculous question — of course I think in my head!"

Whatever your inner voice might have said, it's okay. Just notice it. Since this chapter is all about awareness, our only aim here is to raise our awareness by exploring the place where we tend to spend much of our time: in our heads. Most people typically experience an ongoing stream of thoughts and feelings in the mind — a series of opinions, judgments, positions, evaluations, comparisons, and overall emotional tone which often combine together as a distinct inner voice.

Have you ever noticed what your inner voice says? Typically, the voice in your mind speaks in ways that are congruent with a certain field of consciousness. For example, in the energy field of *anger*, my thoughts and feelings tend to be about anger and its offshoots (irritation, frustration, annoyance, impatience), and my inner voice sounds angry: "That jerk just tried to cut me off!" Similarly, in the energy of love, I tend to feel generous and caring, to think supportive or forgiving thoughts, and to experience an inner voice of loving kindness: "Oh my, that driver seems stressed and hurried — I'll slow down to let him merge into this lane."

If you're like most people, you've probably also developed habitual ways of thinking and feeling that reinforce your usual state of consciousness. This self-talk generally matches your false selves, your masks and acts. What habits and patterns do you notice? Is your inner voice predominantly positive or negative? Is it accepting or critical? Friendly or unfriendly? Frequently it turns out that our habitual inner voice tends to be quite negative, silently speaking in harsh terms. There is an expression that captures this tendency of the mind: *If I had a friend who treats me the way I treat myself, they wouldn't be my friend for long!*

Unfortunately, though, much of our identity is wrapped up in this inner voice that supports our survival strategies. We tend to believe this voice is who we are, since it provides a running commentary on all our experience. When I believe "I am my experience" then I will quite naturally self-identify with the voice in my head that processes and expresses a distilled version of that experience. But identifying with this voice can be problematic and stressful, especially if the mind is tending toward negativity.

There are other traits of the mind that prove challenging, too. It has a tendency to dwell on the past and worry about the future, thus diverting attention from the present moment. It is also easily distracted, switching from one random thought to the next. It can be noisy and turbulent, and likes to make up stories and drama to entertain itself. It is frequently forgetful and unfocused, leading us to operate on a kind of unconscious autopilot. For example, have you ever driven to a destination and, upon arriving, realized you had almost no recollection of the journey? Or, have you ever responded to a simple event, such as the look on someone's face, by creating an epic inner drama—a fabricated story told by the voice in your head that you then got caught up in and started living? These are all examples of unmindfulness, a symptom of unconscious living.

Mindfulness

The good news, however, is that merely observing the mind tends to increase one's consciousness. We can cultivate greater presence and attention simply by noticing what's happening in the mind. Many forms of meditation are built around the Buddhist notion of developing *mindfulness*, which simply means an awareness about our experience. This mindfulness is a way of paying attention to whatever is happening in the present moment without getting caught up and embroiled in it. We become watchers of the mind, putting our inner voice in brackets and allowing us to observe it without judgment. We simply notice what is happening for us in the present moment.

Although this may sound too simple to be helpful, it is actually enormously beneficial. For thousands of years such practices of observing the mind have formed integral parts of various spiritual traditions, and in recent decades mindfulness-based approaches have become increasingly popular in the West as scientific research continues to validate their effectiveness in reducing stress and promoting well-being. For example, Mindfulness Based Stress Reduction (MBSR) and Mindfulness Based Cognitive Therapy (MBCT) are two established, secular mindfulness practices that have become increasingly recognized as effective in helping address a wide range of medical (physiological and psychological) conditions.

Without awareness (i.e. without being conscious and mindful) of our experience, we can't be fully authentic. To grow on our spiritual journey, we need to be mindful of what's happening for us. This is the first step in embracing experience. One way to get more in touch with our experience is simply to notice the voice in our head and to try to understand the thoughts, feelings, and sensations that accompany what it says.

As you become more aware of your inner voice, you may discover that it sounds very different at times, taking on wildly varying tones and styles. The associated emotions and opinions your inner voice expresses might be radically different, or even polar opposites. In fact, if you observe the mind without judgment by noticing the inner voice, you may realize that instead of just one voice in your head, there's actually many voices, many different selves, some shouting loudly in the foreground of awareness, some whispering quietly in the background. Each of these distinct personalities occupies some part of our psychic landscape.

Our Many Selves

If the idea of hearing voices in your head conjures up images of psychiatric wards or crazy people talking to themselves and leaves you feeling threatened, skeptical, or a little anxious...just notice that experience. Or maybe it seems humorous, curious, or a touch absurd. As you read this section, keep noticing your experience. Be mindful of it. That'll help you keep an open mind.

First, let's review what we've covered so far in this chapter. Awareness is the basis of consciousness, and on the human spectrum there are many broad levels of consciousness available to experience. These invisible energy fields color our perceptions by populating our awareness with the thoughts, feelings, and images (forms of experience) that prevail at the level of consciousness we're currently experiencing. The most commonly chosen combinations of these forms become established energy patterns in consciousness (or, if you prefer, in the collective unconscious), each of which can be experienced as an inner personality whose language reflects the consciousness out of which it arose.

You might already be familiar with some of these inner personalities: the wounded child, the sadistic judge, the inner critic, the parent, the rebel, the pusher, the loafer, the nurturer, the controller, the adult, the perfectionist, the victim, the warrior, the protector, the seductress, and many more. We have many such energy patterns, many subpersonalities, inside of us.

This realization leads to two questions: Where do all these unique subpersonalities come from? And how do we deal with them?

For our purposes, the second question is the more important and we'll pursue it shortly. As to the first, psychologists have proposed various concepts (archetypes, complexes, and so on) to explain the origins of these patterns in our personal and collective unconscious. In his book *Subpersonalities—The People Inside Us,* British psychologist John Rowan identified at least six sources of subpersonalities, including the collective, cultural and personal unconscious, dualistic problems or conflicts, the roles we play, and fantasy images that we adopt.

Back in Chapter 1 we touched on one of these sources of subpersonalities in discussing the various masks we wear and the roles we play. We create fictional characters and act out their parts as a way to survive in the world with our inherent vulnerability. But these personalities aren't exclusively our own creations fabricated out of nothing. Though we may have observed many variations of them in the world before adopting them as our own, they actually exist as established energy patterns in consciousness that we merely tune into, drawing them into our minds and making relatively minor alterations to the basic templates in order to create our many selves.

And so, strange as it may seem, we have an inner family of subpersonalities all living under one roof. Through repeated choice and conditioning, we come to identify more with certain subpersonalities than with others and these dominant subpersonalities take over, operating on unmindful autopilot. When this happens, we're not living consciously but are being run by the energy patterns. Occasionally, one of the non-dominant or denied subpersonalities might suddenly speak up and take over, leading to unusual behavior or external events that we're hard pressed to explain because they are so out of character. You may have heard someone say, "I don't know what happened; that wasn't like me at all."

Let's move on to the second question—what should we do about these many selves?

To begin, just notice them. Perhaps this answer comes as no surprise since this is the chapter on awareness. Like any form of experience, we can effectively handle experiencing all these personalities using the ABCs of authenticity, starting with becoming aware of them as they operate in us. But we first need to realize that they're there. As psychologists Hal and Sidra Stone explain in *Embracing Our Selves: The Voice Dialogue Manual*:

> We never realize that our life is being lived for us by an energy pattern that dominates us. The answer to this dilemma is consciousness: being aware of these energy patterns. Consciousness is simply an awareness and experience, and these bring with them the possibility of choice.

In other words, once we become aware of our experience of having many selves within us, it becomes possible to choose consciously how to respond to them.

Each subpersonality—just like each level of consciousness—has something unique to offer us and to teach us, if we will choose to honor it. Honoring a subpersonality, however, doesn't mean letting it take over (since we wouldn't want to literally act out some of our darker subpersonalities) but it does mean (as in Voice Dialogue or some aspects of Gestalt therapy) experiencing it in full awareness so it has a chance to be heard. This allows its energy to be integrated into our lives in a healthy way.

For example, if my playful inner child has been denied and repressed, I may need to learn to reconnect with it and hear its voice in order to bring a childlike, playful spontaneity back into my life. Or, if I've disowned my natural protector or warrior, I may need to reconnect with those energy patterns in order to be able to tap my inner strength and stand up for myself or set healthy boundaries.

Inner Conflict

As with any family, sometimes conflict arises between members living under one roof. You may have noticed a certain type of stress or tension that occurs when different subpersonalities compete for psychic space inside you. These voices can get pretty loud and it can feel like you're at war within yourself. You have an idea about something and you quickly hear a variety of voices: "That's a great idea!", "No it's not!", "What will they think?", "But it could be fun!", "Forget it, it's too risky!" Without awareness to shed light on this inner conflict and illuminate what's going on, coping with it can be enormously painful and difficult.

For example, in response to a challenging life situation or important decision, it is possible that my dominant controller-self may feel threatened and fearful, wanting to minimize risk and uphold its favorite mask of perfection to maintain the *Mr. Know It All* act. At the same time, my adventurous/explorer-self, which might have been denied for years, could feel resentful and angry because it feels stuck in a rut and wants to pursue this new opportunity to embrace change. Meanwhile, my inner critic might be running amok, reminding me of all the ways I am inadequate or incapable of dealing with this situation. Meanwhile, several other subpersonalities on my *inner committee* might be clamoring to speak, too. (What subpersonalities in you have been speaking as you read this?)

With mindfulness, I can learn to notice these inner voices and hear what each is saying without believing any one of them speaks the absolute truth. This helps me integrate the wisdom of each energy into a balanced perspective. Once a voice has been acknowledged, it no longer dominates me and determines my behavior, but I become conscious of it, and free to choose my actions. It comes as a relief to realize that these voices are mine to experience, but they aren't *me*.

Outer Conflict

In real relationships and especially in families, conflict often results as people with different personalities, different masks, different acts, different perspectives, and different priorities—possibly all coming from different paradigms of consciousness—try to share the same space. Navigating these complex interactions can occasionally be a real test of conscious living. As contemporary American spiritual teacher Ram Dass once quipped, "If you think you're so enlightened, go and spend a week with your parents!" (And if that goes well, I would add, then invite your in-laws!)

Through relationships, inner subpersonalities come out to play, although they don't always play nice. Not uncommonly, the same internal conflicts that are happening within you get externalized in your relationships. The very thing that triggers you or upsets you in someone else is a reflection of a conflict that's already happening inside yourself. Just imagine not one but two inner committees colliding in your interactions with another person. Without mindfulness (conscious awareness), any inner war being waged inside of you will also show up as an outer war with the people around you. As we said in Chapter 2, anything unhealed and unhandled within you will eventually show up in your life so you can deal with it. Dealing with differences in relationships is an incredible opportunity to get real about what's really happening inside you.

Relationships are incredibly powerful vehicles for self-realization because in relationships differences get magnified—*greatly* magnified. Such differences can be the source of painful conflict and disagreement that pushes people apart, or they can form the basis of attraction and a richness of interaction that draws them together. With mindful awareness, you reclaim the power to choose how you deal with differences and with conflict. In authentic relationships, all conflict becomes an opportunity for greater closeness and connection.

Awareness and Anxiety

Before we end this chapter, I want to offer a word of warning about all this new self-awareness we've been encouraging.

Becoming aware of new dimensions of our experience can be deeply unsettling or feel overwhelming at first. It's a lot to process. For example, it can be unsettling to realize that your life has been driven by *getting*. It can also be disconcerting to discover you have many subpersonalities within you, some of which have been denied, repressed, or disowned because they didn't fit with the approved self-concept you created to help you survive in the world. Just as certain emotions don't fit with the persona (mask) you developed, certain subpersonalities—especially those that express forbidden emotions—are equally threatening when they emerge in awareness. Thus, we feel anxious.

The American existential psychiatrist, Irvin D. Yalom, observed this phenomenon, noting, "One of the great paradoxes of life is that self-awareness breeds anxiety." Anxiety commonly accompanies increasing self-awareness because those aspects of one's authentic self now being recognized often threaten one's approved self-concept. Any experience that seems similar to the ones you had to defend against during your childhood vulnerability will inevitably stress the persona you created to protect yourself. Indeed, permitting this new awareness may feel like a *return* to that period of excruciating vulnerability and powerlessness against experience. This is the vulnerability problem all over again. Thus, in bringing awareness to our experience, alarm bells sound.

Intellectually, of course, we may now realize these inner alarms are hooked up to outdated security systems based on the survival strategies of a false self. They are a defense against our authentic self and the truth of our experience. But when the alarm bells sound, this perfectly reasonable explanation may seem small comfort against a rising tide of anxiety.

So much of personal growth depends on the willingness to tolerate this temporary anxiety—and on the ability to soothe yourself in the face of it—until the inner conflict is resolved. Through a shift of consciousness, the sense of self expands, the current threat to self disappears, anxiety recedes, and new options emerge.

Until that happens, however, there is the danger of turning to unconscious defense mechanisms and unhealthy coping strategies to deal with one's anxiety. Unfortunately, any mechanism that reduces anxiety by diminishing self-awareness does so at a cost to one's authentic self. As we saw in Chapter 1, the cost of strategies that obscure the authentic self is a loss of meaningful connection in relationships, and of fulfillment in life.

In the next chapter, we'll look at some common coping strategies—including distraction, numbing, and substitution—that inhibit growth and preclude authentic living. In Part II, you'll also learn simple practices for being with any experience in awareness, which helps keep you in the process until the experience is transcended.

> *At the center of your being you have the answer; you know who you are and you know what you want.*
>
> – Lao Tzu

Chapter 4: *B* is for Being

Awareness alone is not enough for genuine living. Although authenticity often begins in awareness, it also requires *being*. We must bring the power of our being to bear in embracing experience. But what does this mean? And how can we go about it? That's what this chapter explores.

At one level, *being* means not being taken over, or taken out, by one's experience. It implies a state of conscious awareness and the ability to remain present with what one is experiencing, responding proactively rather than reactively to what's happening. This response-ability comes largely from taking ownership of one's experience and reclaiming the role of author in one's life.

For me, *being* also implies existence. As a spiritual being having a human experience, I believe the power of your being resides in spirit, where you exist forever. You have, in being, all the spiritual power you need to handle your earthly experience. The human spirit can triumph over the most appalling circumstances and achieve most extraordinary things.

In Chapters 1 and 2, we introduced the twin parts of embracing experience: handling existing experience and creating new experience. We also outlined the A→B→C sequence for each of these, where the 'B' that stands for *being* takes on a slightly different meaning in each case.

Aware of my experience → *Being with it fully* → *Communicating assertively*

Aware of what I value in my Self → *Being those qualities* → *Communicating my Self powerfully*

In handling experience, *being* primarily means *being with*. It means activating the power to fully experience our experience, being with it *as it is* while allowing it into awareness. This way of being with experience, which is a natural ability we all possess, occurs spontaneously when we cease doing the many things that prevent it from happening. Hence, we'll spend much of this chapter becoming familiar with some common defense mechanisms and coping strategies that we use to avoid being with our experience. Also, since so much of our experience is emotional experience, we'll begin this chapter by looking closely at emotions.

In creating experience, *being* means an innate, *spiritual quality of being* that we consciously choose to embody and bring to the world. These are the so-called virtues, spiritual qualities which are revered across diverse cultures as representative of moral excellence and balanced living. We'll look briefly at a sampling of these virtues as part of the *being*-centric paradigm of consciousness we introduced in Chapter 3.

As you may recall, in the Be-Do-Have paradigm, what we do and have flow naturally out of who we choose to be. Often, merely raising our awareness of the many virtuous options available helps us to choose new ways of being. As we own these qualities of our Self by recognizing that they emanate from our spiritual being, we are empowered to bring them into the world.

Authentically embracing experience, in either case, requires taking ownership. First, we must own what's happened and take responsibility for it. Even if what happened occurred in the distant past, perhaps during our excruciating childhood vulnerability, we can choose to be response-able *now*. We can choose how we want to *be with* our experience. Second, we must own the qualities of our Self. We can choose who we want to *be* in the world and thereby create that experience for ourselves. By taking responsible ownership of our lives this way, we powerfully handle the past and are empowered to consciously create the future.

What's an Emotion?

Of all the many kinds of experience, emotions reign supreme. Typically, the loudest and most impactful outer experiences are those that coincide with powerful inner emotions.

Emotionally-based experience tends to be both a driver of behavior as well as its goal. We do things because we *want* to feel a certain way and we do things *because* we feel a certain way. Frequently, emotions trump reason and logic in astonishing and embarrassing ways. How often in your relationships have strong emotions led you to do or say things that you later regretted? How many times have you found yourself acting crazy after getting taken out, or taken over, by reactive emotions? Personally, I've been a raging nut in my relationships more times than I'd like to admit!

At the same time, the most meaningful and fulfilling moments in our lives tend to be deeply emotional. Feelings of joy, pleasure, warmth, and tenderness are all emotional experiences that we long for and cherish. Quickly bring to mind one or two of your most memorable experiences and there is sure to be some strong positive or negative emotion associated with it. (Check in with yourself as you recall these memories: what emotions do you remember experiencing?)

Whenever I speak of *embracing, handling,* or *being with* experience, I am referring mainly to emotional experience. Certainly, it might be necessary for you to learn to deal with the external experience of, say, your mother-in-law (or your boss, spouse, neighbor, etc.), but what you are primarily faced with handling are the emotions that occur inside of you in the context of that relationship. After all, it's never really people or circumstances that are the problem but our emotional reactions to them. If we could handle all the emotions involved, then no problem would remain the same. Indeed, perhaps it wouldn't even exist. So what's the anatomy of an emotion? What's in our emotions that needs to be handled?

Emotion = feeling + thought + sensation

I define an emotion to be a feeling with some thought attached, accompanied by a matching sensation or response in the body. All three experiences occur simultaneously, although, for a few reasons, I like to emphasize *feeling* as the dominant element in the emotional trio.

First, that's how we talk about emotions: "I'm feeling <emotion>." For example, if I say, "I feel scared," you are likely to understand that this emotional experience implies for me a prevailing feeling, one or more associated thoughts, and certain sensations in the body. Second, the experiences we most value or abhor are typically based in feeling. After all, of what value is a happy thought without feeling happy?

To illustrate these three parts of emotion, let's say my current state of consciousness (the tinted perceptual spectacles I'm currently wearing) is based in *having*. This consciousness colors my view of life as being competitive and antagonistic, creating for me a world in which the strong survive by *getting*, using aggression as a primary survival strategy. Emotionally, then, my experience is likely to consist substantially of the feeling we call anger (and its variants: frustration, irritation, impatience, rage, outrage, etc.) with any of an infinite number of supporting angry thoughts attached to that feeling. Matching the feeling and its accompanying thoughts will be an alarm response in the body preparing me to fight, including noticeable sensations such as increased heart rate, flushed skin, and tense muscles. Long-term, remaining in this anger-based consciousness might result in disease in the body, such as a heart *attack*.

This chapter emphasizes emotions, especially the feelings in them, because emotions make up so much of what we need to handle—and *be with*—in our experience. Authentically handling our emotional experience is an essential step in liberating us to create a new experience from a consciousness of *being*.

Emotions Have a Message

I want to emphasize that emotions are neither good nor bad. Each serves an important function in helping us recognize and respond intelligently to our experience in the world. If, for example, I'm standing dangerously close to a cliff's edge or a rattling snake, fear can be an appropriate and helpful emotional signal that helps keep me safe. But this is different from being perpetually frightened and afraid as I go about my day. Similarly, a chronic experience of anger might indicate a lower mode of consciousness, whereas temporary anger can be appropriate and important, even in a higher consciousness, as part of, say, setting a firm and healthy boundary. The same is true of other difficult emotions: grief is appropriate to mourning and guilt can be a guide to conscience. (In Part II, we'll further distinguish natural, healthy emotions).

Emotions have a built-in message telling us something important about ourselves. They say, "Hello! Look over here! Something needs attention!" When we can *be with* the emotions and listen to their message, they can serve our spiritual journey and help us grow. Embracing emotions means we're no longer controlled by them or overwhelmed by them, but we are free to choose how we will *be* in the face of them.

This is a challenging task, however, because emotions carry messages we don't like to hear. They may feel too painful to accept. Some emotions we stuffed away a long time ago because they were overwhelming in our childhood vulnerability (e.g. unresolved trauma). Other emotions clash with our self-concept, threatening to shatter the masks we've carefully constructed to protect us (e.g. if I am *Mr. Nice Guy* then any feeling of anger or upset will threaten my self-image). Anytime these emotions come into awareness, anxiety and stress increase until we can learn to be with all of what's happening inside us.

In order to fully be with feelings, a paradigm of consciousness based in *being* is enormously empowering. Though I may be unable to choose, for example, to be happy or light-hearted when dealing with intense feelings of sadness, there are many qualities of my spiritual being I can align with to support me in handling the sadness authentically, including patience, tolerance, acceptance, and compassion.

I can choose to be kind toward myself and accepting of all my human emotions. After some time, perhaps I can choose to be curious and so inquire, with an adventurous spirit of discovery, into what these emotions are telling me about my life. Finally, I can choose to courageously own these emotions and be responsible for what I've learned from them and what I need to change in me. From there, I can choose what I will communicate and express to others about my lessons and what I am committed to creating in my life.

Elephants and Skeletons

To illustrate the idea of *owning* experience and better distinguish between awareness and being, let's take a stroll through what I call the *house of awareness*.

Like any house, your awareness has many rooms. In each room, there are furnishings, decorations, and prized possessions all representing different forms of experience—thoughts, feelings, memories, and so on. Some of these experiences you like and keep prominently on display, while others you dislike and try to hide away. Because of how awareness works, anything that's in the house is *yours* by definition but it's not *you*. You are the being who lives in the house of awareness while everything in it is simply your experience.

As you move yourself through the house, you bring your being to different parts of your awareness. Just as you likely have favorite rooms in your home to hang out in, you have favorite places to be in your awareness. Some rooms you hardly ever go into, and certain spots in the house are jammed full of experience you rarely deal with (the junk drawer, the storage closet, the attic). And stuff keeps piling up! Mysteriously, the house accumulates dirt and junk unless you regularly visit all parts of the house and clean it up. But to deal with this accumulation of unexperienced experience in your house of awareness, you must first elect to be with it.

As we discussed in Chapter 1, there are certain parts of your experience that don't fit with your idea of who you think you should be, things that you hide away and never let others see. I'm sure you have places in your house you'd be slightly embarrassed to have visitors see, but in the house of awareness the situation is a little more extreme. Like something out of a spooky Halloween tale, you've got a closet nailed shut with wooden boards and yellow tape across it, all covered in cobwebs and a big sign that says, "Do Not Open!!" Hmm, I wonder what's in there?

A skeleton in the closet is any hidden part of your experience you've tried to banish from your awareness, usually because it seemed shameful, fearful, or threatening in some way. You tried to keep it out of awareness by hiding it behind closed doors in the deep recesses of your subconscious mind. In your vulnerable childhood, for example, any experience that you couldn't handle you stuffed into such a closet, slammed the door shut, and boarded it up. You secretly hoped that if you left it there long enough, it would eventually decompose and disappear.

But *unexperienced* experience doesn't disappear on its own, so those skeletons of trauma, terror, and guilt remain lurking just out of awareness. Hidden in the dark, they start to gain a secret power, coming to life and rattling around in the background of awareness. Eventually, these skeletons can no longer be contained, breaking out into conscious awareness, growing bigger by the minute, chasing you around the house, and demanding that you deal with them. Finally, a skeleton gets so big…it turns into an elephant.

An elephant in the room is any sizeable experience of which you are aware, but with which you are refusing to be. You know that it's there (it's pretty hard to overlook and certainly won't fit in any closet) but you simply can't bring yourself to be in the same room with it for long. Instead, anytime you notice this elephant in the room, you quickly look the other way or scoot past it to another room to avoid being with it.

Of course, you may have many reasons and justifications for avoiding an elephant. You think: *it might trample me, there's not enough time, it's too big to handle, other things need my attention, I don't know what to do about it, people will judge me if they see my elephant, it won't change anything,* and so on. In the meantime, however, the elephant takes up a lot of valuable space, making you a prisoner in your own mind. Oh, and it routinely *shoulds* in your house. Actually, there's *should* all over the place. You encounter thought-droppings all over the house, such as: *this shouldn't be happening, I shouldn't have to experience this, it should've gone away by now, I should never have…,* and *I should really shoot this bloody elephant!*

Elephants and skeletons make for poor housemates. They symbolize our internal resistance to experiences which are already *ours* (because they're in our house of awareness), but that we haven't taken complete ownership of. Dealing authentically with these experiences always requires us to bring them out of the darkness and into the light of awareness by allowing ourselves to be with them fully. When we do, they often miraculously transform.

Resistance is Futile

The nature of consciousness is to expand. As a spiritual being, you're here to evolve in consciousness and to realize your fullest potential. If an experience is essential for your spiritual growth, it will not be denied. Anything blocking your growth, anything unhealed or incomplete in you that needs attention, will eventually demand your attention through the circumstances and events in your life. If it isn't dealt with on the inside, it'll keep showing up on the outside. Whatever you refuse to own in your house of awareness will eventually show up in your life. As the saying goes: *what you resist persists.*

Resisting experience, especially emotions, is ultimately a losing game. But that never stops us from trying! In fact, we've developed an impressive arsenal of authenticity defense mechanisms to either diminish our awareness of our experience or prevent us from being with it. In the next section, we'll look at just a few of these mechanisms used to protect our false, ego-based selves and disconnect us from our authentic self.

As you read the next few sections, I invite you to simply notice and be with anything that you recognize about your own life. Doing so will help you avoid creating further resistance as you become aware of any unconscious defenses or unhealthy coping habits operating in you.

Defense Mechanisms

Since emotions consist of feelings, thoughts, and sensations, we tend to develop emotional defenses at all three levels.

With feelings, probably the most common defense is to repress them, to push them down inside of us. Dr. Phil McGraw provides a vivid metaphor for this mechanism in terms of an emotional beach ball. Imagine being in a pool and trying to hold a beach ball under water. The beach ball's tendency is to pop up from beneath the surface and it requires a lot of energy and attention to hold it down. By pushing the ball down, I believe I'm controlling my emotions when, in fact, they're controlling me! I'm not free to have fun in the pool because I spend all my time and energy managing the beach ball. Eventually this task proves exhausting and the beach ball will knock me off balance and come shooting up with force!

Taking this metaphor a step further, imagine the beach ball is striped with rainbow colors, each representing a different emotion. Just as I can't selectively repress feelings, I can't push down just one stripe on the ball—I have to push down all my feelings. Hence, in pushing down anger, fear, or guilt, I also end up pushing down love, joy, and aliveness.

Typically, whatever we repress and deny in ourselves, we then also try to get rid of by unconsciously projecting it onto others. When I project something from my awareness, I secretly tell myself, "This aspect of me isn't okay. It doesn't fit with my mask. I need to get rid of it to be safe, so I'll project it onto someone else. If I see it in them, I don't have to see it in me." Perhaps the forbidden experience is some instinctual impulse, or a strong emotion, maybe even a certain subpersonality. Once we've painted our perception of other people with our forbidden inner experience, we then feel justified in attacking them for possessing the reprehensible trait. Such an attack solidifies our defense against what we refuse to own in ourselves. After all, the best defense is a good offense!

When you encounter someone who you simply cannot tolerate and who triggers you emotionally, there is a very good chance he or she embodies some aspect of yourself that you've disowned. For example, I used to be enormously triggered by talkative women. When I'd be in the company of a Chatty Cathy, I would quietly fume, "Silence, woman! What you're saying makes no sense. How can you blather on about all kinds of feelings without stopping to think about what you're saying?! Get me out of here!" The fact was, I had completely disowned my feeling, feminine side and I adamantly refused to own the fact that I talked incessantly inside my own head. So when I perceived those traits externalized in the world, I would react judgmentally as a defense against acknowledging what I wasn't comfortable with in me.

Psychologically, we also defend ourselves by using thoughts to rationalize, intellectualize, minimize, or explain away anything in awareness that's painful. Similarly, we avoid taking ownership of our experience through complaining, blaming, and excuse-making. Thoughts argue endlessly with reality. Judgments stand in opposition to what is, trying to push it away or change it without first having to accept it and be with it.

At the physical level, we defend against our experience by trying to control the responsive state of the body. One popular survival strategy is *tensing in anticipation of pain*. Holding tension in the body is a means of resisting feelings that we don't want to feel, of clamping down and not letting the emotional energy move freely in us, usually because we anticipate pain. Sometimes it means the emotions get stuffed into our cells, where they're stored in cellular memory until we finally deal with them, perhaps years or decades later.

Of course, tensing the body is an instinctual response when you need to react quickly or when bracing for physical impact. It might make sense if you're about to be attacked by a tiger in the jungle or falling off your bike. Preparing to react and/or bracing for emotional impact, however, when you anticipate being assailed by feelings is unlikely to assist you in, say, having an authentic conversation with your spouse or your boss. In those cases, breathing and releasing the tension will probably serve you better.

Frequently, tension is held in the neck, back, jaw, and shoulders. I can usually measure my body tension by how high my shoulders have climbed up toward my ears. When I find myself hunched up and my neck seems to have disappeared, I know there's some inner stressor or resistance that I've not examined. Another common tensing technique is to tighten the muscles around the chest and stomach, leading to shallow breathing or even holding the breath. Do a quick scan of your tension level right now. Where does it show up? What's your personal tension barometer?

Coping Strategies

When the foregoing basic defense mechanisms prove inadequate to keep us safe from a rising tide of awareness, we may combine them with unconscious coping strategies related to our lifestyle choices. Ironically, we may not even realize that many of our life decisions are unconsciously driven by the need to cope with our inner experience. What kinds of things do we do in order to protect ourselves from our emotions?

We Distract

In our modern world, especially in the West, this generally means keeping busy. *Really busy.* Life happens at a frantic pace that is always on-the-go, keeping our sensory organs stimulated and our awareness preoccupied. We never slow down, even for a minute, lest our emotional experience catch up with us. This means keeping a full schedule, always having things to do and places to go. Even so-called down time is filled up with distractions: movies, TV shows, video games, the internet, sporting events, travel destinations, etc. Unconsciously, we try to manage anxiety by distracting ourselves from the elephants and skeletons in our house of awareness.

We Numb

When distraction alone fails to help us avoid what we're feeling, we try to selectively numb our experience. If our emotional beach ball won't stay below the surface, then we turn to drugs, alcohol, caffeine, sugar, and other substances to help numb feelings we don't want to have. And often they work... *temporarily*. But these self-prescribed medications usually come at a price, frequently making us feel worse than before and requiring more and more of them to continue numbing our escalating emotions.

As a society, we also collectively numb our sensitivity to feelings, especially pain, through routine exposure to violence via entertainment and the media. This desensitization, as it is called, means we become less aware of, and responsive to, painful experiences in ourselves and in others, thereby eroding our capacity for empathy and compassion.

We Substitute

Emotional numbness eventually leads to feeling empty inside. Cut off from the whole of our experience, we're somehow left with a big, empty hole inside. This emptiness comes from being disconnected from our authentic selves. Without a vital connection to our spiritual *being*, we feel unfulfilled inside. Thus, we try to fill up from the outside with substitutes.

Some of the most common substitutes we rely on are the same things that help us distract or numb our feelings (work, movies, TV, alcohol, drugs, sweets, and so on). As I consume more of these substitutes and realize my inner experience remains unchanged, I may begin making even bigger life substitutions in an attempt to fix my predicament: I change jobs, buy a new car, move to a new city, swap-out my partner for a younger version, or have an affair. Yet somehow, as many times as I make substitutions in my life, certain experiences seem to persist.

ॐ

I believe it's important to emphasize here that these coping strategies aren't inherently wrong or bad. It can be healthy to substitute behaviors (e.g. to choose exercise instead of smoking or fighting with a spouse), appropriate to numb (e.g. when getting a root canal), and helpful to use distractions (e.g. from an ongoing stressful situation or major life crisis). There's also nothing wrong with a full, busy life. Nor is there anything intrinsically bad about entertainment, coffee, alcohol, drugs, or a new relationship. They all have their place. What's important is to make conscious choices about what purpose all these things serve in creating the life we want to live. If we are using or abusing them to avoid dealing with our experience they will disconnect us from our authentic self and inhibit personal and spiritual growth.

Resistance, whether through defense mechanisms or coping strategies, is futile. As we said earlier, anything unhealed or incomplete inside of you will eventually show up outside of you in order to help you face it. Whatever lessons are needed for your spiritual growth *will* recur until learned. Skeletons and elephants *will* remain in the house until we get real about them, meeting them in awareness with the full power of our being.

The Power of Being

As a spiritual being, you have access to all the power you need to triumph over your experience. Instead of being helplessly pushed around by your experience, unconsciously driven to defend against it or merely struggling to cope with it, you have enormous power to transform and transcend your experience. You might be faced with difficult or painful challenges and you may have been wronged or hurt in this life, but you are not powerless.

To be vulnerable doesn't mean to be powerless. Remember, in your human experience you're *inherently* vulnerable. You don't get to choose most of what happens in the world and you don't get to control everything that comes into your awareness. Your real freedom lies in how you choose to *be with* what happens, and who you elect to be through the choices you make. Vulnerability is not victimhood—you always have the power to choose your response to life.

Following the Second World War, Viktor Frankl, an Austrian psychiatrist and Holocaust survivor, wrote about his experiences as a concentration camp inmate and his belief that man, even in the face of the most extreme suffering, can find meaning and a sense of responsibility in life:

> *Ultimately, man should not ask what the meaning of his life is, but rather he must recognize that it is he who is asked. In a word, each man is questioned by life; and he can only answer to life by answering for his own life; to life he can only respond by being responsible.*

> *We who lived in concentration camps can remember the men who walked through the huts comforting others, giving away their last piece of bread. They may have been few in number, but they offer sufficient proof that everything can be taken from a man but one thing: the last of the human freedoms—to choose one's attitude in any given set of circumstances, to choose one's own way.*

> *We must never forget that we may find meaning in life even when confronted with a hopeless situation, when facing a fate that cannot be changed. For what then matters is to bear witness to the uniquely human potential at its best, which is to transform a personal tragedy into a triumph, to turn one's predicament into a human achievement. When we are no longer able to change a situation we are challenged to change ourselves.*

To live consciously means to continuously choose one's response to life. Free will *is* this freedom of response-ability that belongs to you as a spiritual being. Inner triumph occurs anytime you choose, from within your authentic self, a way of being that realizes your uniquely human potential. In exercising this power, outer circumstances can and often do change — they transform. Those situations, however, that *cannot* be changed can still be transcended, requiring that *we* transform.

Taking ownership of one's experience and handling it authentically using the ABCs of authenticity catalyzes this transformation, this shift in consciousness. I define responsibility as the ownership of the capacity for choice. Spiritually, this means exercising free will. Your free (spiritual) will is exercised by setting an intention to align with and become those qualities of your (spiritual) being that you value most. To truly value something is to choose it; and in choosing it one becomes it. Referring to a consciousness of *being*, author and spiritual teacher David R. Hawkins states, "Your greatest gift to the world lies not in what you say or do, but in what you have become."

Virtues

To become what you value most guarantees a genuine life. So who do you aspire to be? What qualities of being do you value? What guides your life and makes it flourish? If you don't know, you won't grow!

Any quality that is deemed to be morally good and is valued as promoting individual and collective well-being is known as a virtue. Whether identified by long-standing religious authorities or through recent research in positive psychology, virtues are remarkably consistent across cultures and are generally accepted as the basis of a good life. Not surprisingly, these virtues also match the experiences we tend to value most.

Benjamin Franklin — one of the Founding Fathers of the United States and an author, scientist, inventor, political theorist, businessman, diplomat and more — is an inspiring and very human example of virtuous living. In 1726, at the age of 20, Franklin developed a plan to cultivate 13 virtues that he practiced in some way for the rest of his life. He would focus on a single virtue every week, thus completing a course in his 13 virtues four times in each year. Although he didn't always, by his own admission, live up to his chosen virtues, he felt the attempt made him a better and happier man, contributing greatly to his success.

On the next page are one hundred virtues for you to review and consider, courtesy of The Virtues Project™.

Of course, this is only a partial list to whet your creative appetite. There are variations and combinations of these virtues that can be expressed in other words which might appeal to you better. For example, other qualities you might choose to embrace include being bold, expressive, warm, calm, clear, vulnerable, tender, imaginative, polite, rational, easy-going, or humorous! Perhaps you'd like to experience more energy, vitality and aliveness, or adopt a playful spirit of discovery toward life and relationships. There are no limits to what you can create!

As you review these possibilities, you might also discover that you already embody certain virtues or qualities very well. They seem a natural part of your character and you can easily bring them into your experience anytime you choose. You may even be known among your friends and family for possessing certain traits. Other virtues, however, might represent growth opportunities for you. Several qualities may not match your current persona or self-concept, and so present a challenge for you to consciously embrace. Indeed, it might feel somewhat vulnerable to bring these qualities into your life.

Take a moment now to note which virtues you identify with and which ones seem unfamiliar or challenging. What qualities would you like to create as a regular part of your experience? Which ones would serve you in your current relationships? Which ones are you committed to embodying?

Being in Relationship

Nowhere is your power of being more likely to be tested than in relationships. The closer the relationship, the more likely

Acceptance	Fidelity	Peacefulness
Accountability	Flexibility	Perceptiveness
Appreciation	Forbearance	Perseverance
Assertiveness	Forgiveness	Prayerfulness
Awe	Fortitude	Purity
Beauty	Friendliness	Purposefulness
Caring	Generosity	Reliability
Certitude	Gentleness	Resilience
Charity	Grace	Respect
Cheerfulness	Gratitude	Responsibility
Cleanliness	Helpfulness	Reverence
Commitment	Honesty	Righteousness
Compassion	Honor	Sacrifice
Confidence	Hope	Self-discipline
Consideration	Humanity	Serenity
Contentment	Humility	Service
Cooperation	Idealism	Simplicity
Courage	Independence	Sincerity
Courtesy	Initiative	Steadfastness
Creativity	Integrity	Strength
Decisiveness	Joyfulness	Tact
Detachment	Justice	Thankfulness
Determination	Kindness	Thoughtfulness
Devotion	Love	Tolerance
Dignity	Loyalty	Trust
Diligence	Mercy	Trustworthiness
Discernment	Mindfulness	Truthfulness
Empathy	Moderation	Understanding
Endurance	Modesty	Unity
Enthusiasm	Nobility	Wisdom
Excellence	Openness	Wonder
Fairness	Optimism	Zeal
Faith	Orderliness	
Faithfulness	Patience	

you are to be tested in your ability to remain conscious and present, especially as emotional intensity increases. As limitless vehicles for self-realization, relationships can be quite humbling in the many ways they confront us with growth experiences, and challenge our commitment to a conscious, virtuous life.

For real relationships to flourish, the power of *being* is absolutely required. Often, the surest way to water any relationship and help it grow is simply to *be with* the other person in their world, without judging, evaluating, or otherwise resisting what they are experiencing and expressing. In the coaching work I do with couples, the single most important communication skill they work to develop is this capacity to *be* in the presence of their partner and to connect deeply and empathically with them in their inner world.

An empathic connection and understanding necessarily implies awareness and recognition of emotions. Emotions, as we saw earlier in this chapter, comprise so much of our inner experience. When I can recognize the emotional truth of another, and relate it sensitively back to what I know of those emotions from my own experience, then I open the door to a compassionate understanding of what's really happening for that person.

In fact, dealing authentically with someone else's experience requires applying the ABCs of authenticity in much the same way as when we handle our own experience: by (A) becoming aware of what's happening for them, (B) being fully present with them, and (C) listening empathically to what they are communicating. When the other person senses someone really *gets* them, the relationship will often transform.

One of the ways you can help others get real with their experience and share it vulnerably and responsibly with you is by choosing to embody virtues that create a sacred space in which they feel heard, valued, respected, and appreciated. You can draw upon whatever spiritual qualities in your Self are needed to create this space and bring acceptance, kindness, patience, or self-discipline to the process.

Some great questions to ask when facing an emotionally-charged relationship situation include:

- Could I be with this situation without wanting to change or control it?
- How do I want to be with this person?

- What quality of being can I bring to this situation?
- What's missing here? What's needed that I can provide?
- What virtue or quality would serve best here?
- If I were the embodiment of that quality (kind, loving, generous, assertive) how would I respond?

These questions naturally invite ownership of the situation and empower you to deal with it authentically. Taking ownership of any experience you're presented with and reclaiming the power to author how you'll respond to it is an empowering approach to relating.

100% Responsibility: Good Own-Ya!

To end this chapter, I want to encourage you to exercise the power of your being in two simple words: *own everything*.

Whatever arises in awareness for you to experience, own it. Be with it. Whenever you notice a pattern in your relationships, own it. Own your emotions. Own your defense mechanisms. Own your coping strategies. Own your animal nature. Own everything: you have enough spiritual power to handle it all.

At the same time, take ownership of your greatness. Own the innate qualities of your spiritual being. Own your courage. Own your compassion. Own your eternal, conscious, blissful nature. These virtues all emanate from your true Self and will show up in your experience as you choose and affirm them. Also own your creation of sacred space anytime you help someone feel heard. Own your capacity to be with them in that way.

Practice owning everything. Anytime you own something, recognize yourself for it by saying, "Good own-ya, mate!" Have some fun with this! Go ahead and say it with a thick Australian accent. Get a little silly if you like and invite your friends to join you. Each time you authentically *handle* or *create* an experience, celebrate! High-five a friend or give yourself a pat on the back for taking ownership of your life. This will reinforce your personal responsibility, affirming your capacity to live a genuine life.

A standpoint of one hundred percent (100%) personal responsibility means being the author of one's experience of life through the power of choice. Owning your *response-ability* means taking ownership of this capacity for choice. Although you cannot decide or control everything that happens in your life, you can always choose how you will be with it. You *can* choose what you value and respond accordingly. Even when you temporarily disown your power to create your experience, as we all occasionally do, you can still choose to authentically handle *that* experience and be responsible for it.

Embracing one hundred percent responsibility in relationships is especially empowering and liberating. We can consciously assert, "I am one hundred percent responsible for my experience in this relationship. My experience depends one hundred percent on me and my choices, and *zero* percent on the other person." This is a major departure from most victim-based relationship paradigms in which we give our power away completely to the other person to determine our experience based on whether or not they meet our needs. The paradigm of one hundred percent responsibility is also not a fifty-fifty, *tit-for-tat* paradigm in which our experience depends on a continuous bartering of love, and the phrase, "I love you very much," really means, "I trade you very much." When taking ownership of, and one hundred percent responsibility for, our experience in relationship, we are free to love one hundred percent of the time.

Of course, this doesn't mean we never take actions to improve a relationship, or even leave an unhealthy one. Being unconditionally loving doesn't mean being an unconditional doormat, or a "love-victim." Rather, it means we're at choice about our attitude and behavior and we can take action from a consciousness of *being* in which we've chosen to be compassionate, kind, loving, and respectful—toward both our self and the other person. One hundred percent responsibility also doesn't mean we hide our true feelings behind a mask of inauthentic spirituality because we now think we *should* be happy one hundred percent of the time. That's only a further denial of our full authentic self. Rather, when we own our response-ability, we're free to choose our response even to difficult emotions, and to handle them authentically with the ABCs.

~

And so: *Good own-ya* for reading this far and for reclaiming the power to triumph in your life!

In this chapter, you explored the power of your (spiritual) being and learned the importance of being with your experience as part of handling it authentically. You also learned the anatomy of an emotion and strolled through the house of awareness. You identified some of the defense mechanisms and coping strategies that you use to resist being with your experience, you got in touch with the virtues and spiritual qualities that are important for who you want to be, and you learned the importance of taking ownership of all of it from a standpoint of one hundred percent personal responsibility.

In the previous two chapters, you've taken a whirlwind tour of the 'A' and the 'B' in the ABCs of authenticity. You learned that *awareness* and *being* make possible a conscious existence, giving you the power to fully embrace both handling and creating your experience as part of your spiritual journey. In the next chapter, we'll look at how to harness this authentic power by taking ownership of your self-expression through empowered *communication*.

*The single biggest problem with communication is
the illusion that it has taken place.*

– George Bernard Shaw

Chapter 5: *C* is for Communication

Communication is the basis of self-expression. To be authentic means to express yourself in a way that is congruent with your *awareness* and *being*, bringing the full power of your authentic self into your relationships. Such empowered communication is characteristically conscious, assertive, and responsible. It allows you to choose to reveal yourself deeply and vulnerably to others, to connect with them in meaningful ways, and to share mutual understanding and empathy.

When you communicate authentically, people *get you*—they understand your experience and are clear about what you want and what you are committed to creating. When you relate without masks and façades, others aren't left wondering about what your experience is or what's really important to you.

In this chapter, we'll look at principles of empowered communication that support real relationships and genuine living. In the practices in Part II of this book, you'll have the opportunity to put some of these principles into action in your life.

You're Always Communicating

Communication is always happening. You're never *not* communicating. Moreover, communication happens on many levels: your actions and decisions, the vibe or energy you give off, visual cues (your body language, posture, eye contact, facial expressions, and so on), paralanguage (your tone of voice, inflection, pacing, emphasis, and more) and, finally, what you say with words.

Indeed, the words you choose, while vitally important, are only one part of what you communicate to others. Often, actions speak louder than words. Similarly, not being genuine in what you say undermines what you're saying.

For example, imagine a husband asking his wife after an argument, "Are you still upset with me?" With her arms crossed, looking away, foot tapping, she responds curtly in a sharp tone, "Nope." Certainly her reply isn't authentic, and even a fairly dense hubby is likely to realize the words aren't congruent with the overall message: emotionally, she's communicating "Yes." Even without words, a seething silence or a steely gaze would probably communicate the same message.

Especially where emotions are involved, we draw most of our conclusions about what's being communicated based on non-verbal signals, not on what is actually said. Whenever words are in conflict with non-verbal cues about emotional reality, we generally believe the non-verbal truth as expressed by facial expressions and tone of voice.

In my relationship, when one of us communicates incongruently this way because we are experiencing an emotion we've not yet taken ownership of, the other person may gently provide an invitation to own it and tell the truth. In the scenario above, that might look like lovingly and playfully inquiring with the other person, "Are you telling me the truth, love?" Because we're committed to the truth in our relationship, this question often gets an equally curt "No" in response, followed by a smile or laughter. Even if it gets an inauthentic "Yes" it still usually gets a laugh and raises awareness. At that point, our communication starts to get real again as defenses are dropped and we're able to approach the emotional elephant in the room. (Amazingly, acknowledging and approaching the elephant is often all that's needed for it to disappear.)

Being authentic means striving to bring your awareness, being, and communication (A→B→C) into alignment with your experience. This means all levels of communication, not just words. Because so much of our experience is emotionally-based, effective communication in relationships usually recognizes and acknowledges emotions. As we'll see shortly, being authentic doesn't always mean I *express* my emotions, but it does mean I own them (they don't own me) and I *can* express them if I choose.

Are You Choosing?

Conscious communication implies choice. It means the freedom to decide how to best express what's happening in your experience for the greatest good of all concerned. How much of what you're (always) communicating are you choosing consciously?

Not uncommonly, our communication decisions are unconscious and conditioned. They're habits we picked up somewhere along the way without too much thought or any training. Often, they're not the most helpful or healthy habits of relating. When our communication is unconsciously driven by the need to uphold a mask for the sake of security, approval, or control, then we're not free to express our authentic self and we inevitably create disconnection in relationships.

In discussing paradigms of consciousness in Chapter 3, we looked at a lower mode of consciousness based in *having*, in which a primary goal is to ensure survival in a hostile world through *getting*. In this mode of consciousness, interpersonal communication is seen primarily as a means of acquisition so that a conversation might conceivably be defined as follows: *a conversation is a vocal competition in which the person catching their breath is called the listener.*

It's a sad fact that many relationship conversations are competitive in nature, with each person locked in a game of one-upmanship trying to argue their position, defend their opinion, have their way, refute the other's point of view, make a witty comeback, look smart, put the other person down, or upstage what's been shared with a more dramatic story. It's a no-holds-barred communication grudge match in which listening is no more than the annoying period of time each opponent spends waiting for the other to shut up in order to resume speaking.

Grim as that depiction may sound, it's a rather commonplace occurrence. I admit, none too proudly, that I've participated in more than a few such vocal competitions over the years and I can confidently say that those non-conversations have never created for me the vulnerable self-expression, deep connection, and ongoing fulfillment I now associate with real relationships.

Fortunately, life gave me several very painful, jarring, and eerily similar experiences that helped increase my awareness about the many unconscious communication habits, patterns, and assumptions that were running my life and ruining my relationships. Thankfully, I found I could choose differently. One of the most enduring and endearing of these lessons about choice was when I finally *got* that effective communication begins with listening—and that by choosing to listen I could transform my relationships.

Try Listening

> *An unhappy couple walks into a marriage therapist's office. Once seated, the therapist asks them, "How can I help you? What seems to be the problem?" Immediately, both husband and wife begin talking over one another and at the therapist, each relaying in angry and resentful tones a similar view that their spouse, effectively, is the problem. After a momentary flurry of chaos and confusing accusations, the therapist interrupts them by holding up his hands and says, "I'm sorry. I believe I asked the wrong question. Let me ask this instead: Who is willing to listen?" An uncomfortable, hostile silence then ensues for the next ten minutes, broken finally by one of the couple who quietly observes, "I think I see the problem."*

Philosopher Paul Tillich once declared, "The first duty of love is to listen." Listening as an act of love brings life to relationships. It begins by directing our conscious presence—our awareness and being—to another person with the intent to understand their experience, especially their emotional experience. This kind of *empathic listening* is an active process of striving to be fully with the other person in their inner world while at the same time not losing one's self in it.

Empathic listening is supported by a joyful spirit of discovery and healthy sense of adventure because it requires leaving behind one's own world (with all of its biases, judgments, and meanings) and entering into a new world, a foreign realm of experience. It means being motivated to discover what's happening in another with no preconceived notions of what will be found there, as well as being secure enough in one's self to sail out into those uncharted waters and risk being buffeted about by the unpredictable forces of experience (tides of feeling, gales of thought, storms of reaction, and more).

This practice is not for the faint of heart! Temporarily suspending judgments and evaluations isn't easy, especially in emotionally-charged situations. Leaving behind the security of cherished views, positions, and opinions is deeply uncomfortable and challenging. Peering through a different lens of perception to come to a clear understanding of the other person's world feels dangerous because if I did, if I was touched and moved by what I discovered there, I might also discover something in *my* world that I need to examine. Worse still, I might realize I need to *change* something in myself or my life based on what I learn—and the threat of change is always a frightening prospect. In short, this kind of listening might be vulnerable!

Genuine listening, therefore, will often trigger insecurity and anxiety as it activates the defense mechanisms of a false self. Unfortunately, those same defense mechanisms also preclude meaningful dialogue and prevent authentic connection between me and the other person, who might just happen to be my spouse, my child, or my best friend. Indeed, the closer I am to the other person, the more difficult listening seems to become.

Nevertheless, empathic listening remains arguably the greatest gift of caring—the first duty of love. Years ago when I first took on a practice of conscious, empathic listening in all my relationships my life changed dramatically. I suddenly had access to whole new worlds of understanding and a veritable wealth of valuable (and valid!) perspectives that enriched my life in countless ways. It wasn't always easy, but I made a wholehearted commitment to understand others through listening.

Before long, listening to my girlfriend, family, friends, teachers, mentors, colleagues, and even strangers on the street became immensely fulfilling and rewarding. It was like discovering a secret way to breathe life into people who'd been slowly suffocating. What joy! Not only did they feel better, but I felt honored and inspired by what they shared with me: their hopes, dreams, problems, fears, triumphs, tragedies, insecurities, joys, regrets, frustrations, buried secrets, terrible losses, fond memories, and incredible stories. It was all so very *real*.

Frequently, I found that by giving my undivided attention to others and listening with my whole being, they very often poured out their hearts. My genuine (if not always graceful) efforts at listening communicated so powerfully to the people around me that they honored me by sharing powerful and profound things about themselves. Inevitably, the vulnerability and genuineness I saw in them also helped me find the courage to discover myself—my own hopes, dreams, fears, losses, and so on.

Now, for the sake of full disclosure, I must admit I didn't always like what I heard. Sometimes what others shared was scary, frustrating, confronting, confusing, annoying, heartbreaking, or gut-wrenching. At times, I wanted to stop and plug my ears. If strong emotions were expressed, I wanted to either attack, defend, or escape. My inner alarm bells rang frequently. Occasionally, I actually did need to step back and take a break from this practice, but more often than not I chose to listen—and I discovered an amazing thing. Frequently, the most trying and difficult experiences (such as those involving anger, criticism, hatred, or rejection), when met with understanding, transformed into the very relationship treasures I now cherish most (deep connection, trust, laughter, and friendship).

Anger and irritation in others—and in me—gave way to hidden feelings of hurt or fear. As façades and fronts crumbled on both sides, our vulnerable admissions then led to the sharing of other suffering and loss. Those experiences, in turn, gave voice to dreams and desires. Sprinkled throughout were incredible memories, hilarious moments, and inspiring stories. All that was needed for me to access these experiences was the willingness to keep listening.

But this kind of listening is not easy: simple, yes, but not easy. It takes practice. More, it requires the power of conscious presence, the full measure of our awareness and being. And, oh, it calls for courage, courage, courage. I find I am as consistently humbled by how greatly the practice of listening challenges my commitment *to* it as I am inspired by how richly it rewards my persistence *with* it.

Anytime the desire to understand exceeds the desire to defend or attack, rewarding and enlivening connection occurs. Dropping masks, suspending judgments, being vulnerable, and striving to empathically understand another's experience with an open heart and open mind opens the door to conscious relating. These things flow naturally out of a consciousness centered in *being*, which provides the spiritual power necessary to stay present in listening and remain connected in relationship.

If I could write one prescription for agonizing symptoms of disconnection in any relationship—be it with Other, Self, or God—it would surely be for a listening pill. "Take two of these and call me in the morning." Without doubt, that has proven good medicine in my life. As an act of love, listening is a practice with unlimited healing potential.

Listen To Yourself

Just as in the previous chapter we saw how relationship conflicts are often an external manifestation of internal conflicts, it's also commonly the case that the capacity to listen to another is a reflection of the capacity to listen to one's self. To the extent that you are aware of your own experience and able to be with it, so too are you able to listen to another person, to be with her in full awareness of her experience. But if you cannot genuinely listen to yourself, it's exceedingly hard to listen empathically to another with any real desire to understand.

If you cannot face your own inner animal, how can you meet it compassionately when it snarls at you through the teeth of another? If you cannot hear the frightened child in you, how will you ever truly listen to the 5-year-old trembling at your feet? If you cannot feel your own anger, hurt, or fear, how will you empathize with those feelings in another? If you cannot recognize your feminine and masculine sides, how can you possibly hope to meet them with understanding when they are animated to life in your partner? Jiddu Krishnamurti expressed it this way: "When I understand myself, I understand you, and out of that understanding comes love."

Listening to understand, as we have described it, is a wellspring of love. And the practice can begin simply by listening to discover yourself. Before listening to another, first ask: Can I wholly receive my authentic self, in the fullness of my experience, without resisting it and making it wrong? Can I *get real* with what's happening inside me by directing my conscious presence with the intent to understand and without immediately judging or evaluating what I discover? Can I bring compassionate acceptance to my own emotions, sub-personalities, limitations, fallibility, and human nature? If I cannot, then this limitation in my internal communication will eventually show up in my relationships as well.

In relationships, external communication breakdowns—the most commonly cited marriage problem—frequently stem from a breakdown of internal communication in one or both individuals. Are you disconnected from large parts of yourself? Are you putting on fronts and holding up masks? How can you possibly expect your partner to know what you feel, what you want, what you value, or what you need if you cannot first connect with those experiences in you? How will he or she ever come to know who you are if you don't know yourself?

If listening is the first duty of love, then to *know thyself* through inner-directed listening is always the primary responsibility on a compassionate journey of self-realization. Although it will confront you with all the same challenges as listening to others (if not more!) the rewards to be reaped on your spiritual journey are well worth the effort.

In the coming sections, we'll turn our attention away from listening in order to explore assertive and responsible self-expression, but I want to emphasize that empowered communication is always based in listening. Please keep this in mind as you read the rest of this chapter. What you say is most powerful when it's real, which it can only be if you've listened deeply to yourself and taken full ownership of your experience. How you then share that experience, of course, also has a profound influence on how others will receive it.

Share Responsibly

Responsible self-expression implies continuously making choices about how to respond to experience, including whether or not to communicate about it and how to do so. In this section we'll take a closer look at these communication choices and highlight the impact they have on relationships.

First, I want to dispel any kindergarten notions that the 'C' in the ABCs of authenticity implies you must communicate every experience you have in order to be authentic. This would hardly be feasible, never mind advisable! Nor does the 'C' imply a kind of free license to irresponsibly blast or bludgeon others with your experience in the name of pseudo-authenticity: "I feel...you're a total jerkface! That's just my experience, okay? Look, I'm just being *real*." Wielding words as weapons of attack or mechanisms of defense is just more antics of a fearful, false self.

Conscious communication involves important choices regarding *if* and *when* to share. There are situations and times in life when the most responsible thing to do is *not* to share your inner experience, at least not immediately. There are also times when failing to communicate your inner experience might be deemed highly irresponsible.

There's no strict set of rules, however, determining when the most responsible choice is to speak up versus when it's better to remain silent; it depends on the individual and the situation. For many people—and often in the context of a coaching relationship—learning to express feelings *more* is an important path of growth and self-realization. However, it is equally possible that for some the crucial lesson lies in learning to curb unhealthy emotional expression and to simply be with those feelings instead (without, of course, repressing or *beach-balling* them). There is as much a place for authentic restraint in responsible communication as there is a place for genuine boldness of expression. The key principle here is being conscious and at choice with respect to sharing our experience, especially our feelings.

Remember, however, that you're always communicating at some level even if you aren't speaking. Thus, if you're aware of an emotion that you're broadcasting nonverbally, it's often helpful to own it by at least acknowledging it verbally: "I feel sad right now and I'm not sure why," or, "I am angry but not yet ready to talk about it. Can I come back in ten minutes?" An authentic acknowledgment of any emotional elephant in the room often prevents a great deal of misunderstanding and miscommunication. Sometimes the experience passes as quickly as it came and there's no need to express yourself. At other times, you might consciously choose to share.

That brings us to the topic of *how* to communicate responsibly once having decided to do so.

Get Consent

One way to support responsible sharing is to seek permission before expressing yourself. For example: "I have something I'd like to share with you—are you willing to listen? Is now a good time?" This simple communication habit creates so much benefit in so few words. First, it declares your intent and desire to share; second, it signals to the other person that she is being asked to listen; and third, it invites her full engagement by giving her a choice to participate or to decline.

You can probably recall a time when someone started expressing themselves to you *without* your consent. How did that feel? How well did you listen? What if their sharing was emotionally-charged or quite negative, perhaps full of complaining or blaming? The experience of someone dumping their negative feelings on you uninvited can be rather unpleasant. It's the emotional equivalent of getting suddenly and unexpectedly puked on: it's messy and it stinks! Sharing without consent can put significant strain on relationships.

Use *I*-Statements

Responsible self-expression also keeps the focus on self and not on others. One way to do this is with the use of *I*-statements instead of *You*-statements. For example, imagine hearing the statements below:

1. You didn't pick me up on time again. You're always late! You're so selfish—you don't care about anyone but yourself.

2. I feel hurt and angry when I wait alone to be picked up. This is the third time this month I've waited for more than 20 minutes and each time I end up thinking I don't matter much to you.

How do you feel or respond when you hear these different modes of self-expression? The first case uses *You*-statements exclusively, revealing little about the speaker's inner experience, except indirectly. It may sound accusatory or antagonistic because of the evaluations and judgments being expressed. The second statement, by contrast, conveys facts and uses only *I*-statements to directly and concretely express the speaker's experience. Which would you prefer to hear?

I-statements reflect responsible ownership of experience, whereas *You*-statements generally deflect ownership and avoid vulnerability by putting the focus elsewhere. The chances of an *I*-statement causing conflict are much less because it's hard to argue with feelings that someone owns and shares responsibly. While *I*-statements may feel more vulnerable, they're also generally more authentic.

Another way to disown experience using *You*-statements (or *We*-statements) is to speak in vague, general terms instead of concrete, personal terms. For example:

3. You know how when someone doesn't do something? And you just end up thinking that you wish they would. Everyone should do those things, I think. We kind of have to…"

This style of communication uses an editorial *you* and *we* commentary with language that is vague and confusing. It's not clear what the speaker is communicating about his personal experience. Would you have understood he was hurt or angry about being picked up late? Speaking in generalities avoids taking ownership of one's experience at the expense of rendering the communication ineffective or impotent.

Responsible sharing draws its potency from the ownership of experience, as reflected by choosing words such as *I, me,* and *my*. When I speak directly and vulnerably about me and my experience, my self-expression becomes powerful and captivating because it's immediate and real. When I declare that *I feel* or *I believe* the message is compelling because it makes a personal revelation. In addition, the more concrete and specific I can be about my experience, the more effective my communication becomes.

Another downside of *You*-statements is their tendency to create reactivity in the listener. Listening is challenging enough in the best of circumstances. It can feel vulnerable and threatening. It can activate defense mechanisms and trigger emotional reactivity. *You*-statements only increase the likelihood that these hindrances to productive and satisfying dialogue will

Responsible Sharing

1. I regret what I said to you. It wasn't kind. I'm sorry.

2. I remember things differently so I am feeling shocked and confused by what I'm hearing.

3. I don't like coming home to dirty dishes in the sink. I feel angry and upset. I would like it if you'd wash your dishes after using them.

4. I've had a stressful and tiring day at work and I'd really like to talk about it. Are you willing to listen?

5. I feel sad and lonely when you don't come home from work until late in the evening and I eat dinner alone.

Other Sharing

C'mon, you know I didn't mean it. You're too sensitive.

Oh, you've got to be joking. You're wrong. That is not what happened!

You're such a slob! You're always leaving dishes for me to wash. You must think I'm your maid!

Ugh, what a day! You'll never guess what happened. Get this. Everyone at work was in a bad mood and ...

You're such a workaholic! You're never here for me when I need you. Don't you love me?

occur. *You*-statements are often perceived as a form of attack or accusation, increasing the chances that the listener will experience some kind of threat, insecurity, defensiveness, or emotional reaction. Read the contrasting statements above and just notice your inner response.

As emotions escalate, the capacity to stay present in conversation rapidly diminishes. At the same time, distortion in the messages and meanings being communicated also increases. *I*-statements help avoid these pitfalls. Responsible self-expression minimizes the listener's sense of threat and ensuing emotional reaction while maximizing his or her chances of hearing and correctly understanding your message. Of course, authentic communication based on responsible sharing doesn't guarantee the listener will accept your message or understand your meaning, however it does make those outcomes much more likely.

Own Your Irresponsible Sharing

There's a very good chance, if you're human, that you'll have times when you share less than consciously and perhaps irresponsibly. Maybe you were triggered emotionally and reacted unconsciously, saying things you didn't mean and now regret. Perhaps you emotionally vomited all over a friend without realizing it or carelessly volunteered your opinion to someone without consent, creating hurt or pain for them in the process. Owning these communication missteps as soon as possible once they happen is an important part of authentic living that helps restore connection and closeness in relationships.

Spoken humbly and from the heart, the words "I'm sorry" are amazingly effective at undoing the negative effects of our less than stellar moments. They can quickly mend ruptured connection caused by emotional reactivity, defensiveness, or attack. Simply dropping a defensive mask of, say, perfection or needing to be right, and vulnerably expressing a decent regret about past choices or behavior revitalizes relationships and keeps them strong.

Missteps *will* happen and it's important to realize they're not the end of the world. Sometimes they provide real opportunities for growth and connection. Initially, it can be uncomfortable to own your missteps, but as you practice you'll eventually learn to deal with them almost as soon as they happen. With conscious presence, you'll hear yourself speak and call out your communication like it is. For example: "Wow, that didn't come out right at all—it sounded condescending and mean. I'm sorry. I'd like to try again. It's important to me to communicate to you with care and respect." Or similarly, "I notice I've been rambling and I didn't even ask if you wanted to hear all this. I'm sorry. I'd really like to express myself more clearly and to feel understood—are you open to me trying again?"

You can even learn to have fun with this process of correction. Go ahead and ask for a communication mulligan or a self-expression do over. See what happens. Most people will respond quite generously when you take ownership of anything defensive, reactive, fake, or phony in your communication and ask them for a second chance. You might even end up sharing a good laugh about it. After all, who among us hasn't made the same mistake at some point? When you ask for forgiveness, you give others a chance to step into their generosity and greatness.

Be Assertive

As you engage in sharing responsibly, including owning any missteps along the way, you'll likely discover that a life filled with real relationships is also filled with opportunities to engage in potentially difficult or challenging conversations. When faced with the prospect of speaking up about something that might be hard for you to say or unpleasant for others to hear, what manner of self-expression is most effective?

Assertiveness is a balanced mode of responsible communication that combines confident, courageous, and bold self-expression with care, consideration, and respect for others. To be assertive means to offer forth one's authentic self in a non-manipulative manner that is neither aggressive nor passive. Assertiveness is helpful in expressing our feelings or views, asking for what we want, communicating our values, setting boundaries, saying no, requesting help, and standing up for ourselves. The table on page 92 compares qualities of assertive, aggressive, and passive modes of expression.

Assertive communication is effective in many situations, including when: something's wrong with your order at a restaurant, a friend who owes you money asks to borrow more, someone in your home isn't respecting the rules of the house, an employee you supervise keeps showing up late to work, your parents want you to fly out for a visit but you don't want to go, you are asked in a job interview why you are the right person for the position, and so on.

Passivity	Assertiveness	Aggressiveness
Afraid	Direct	Threatening
Helpless	Courageous	Abrasive
Anxious	Honest	Harsh
Defeated	Considerate	Insensitive
Insecure	Secure	Cocksure
Weak	Respectful	Loud
Fragile	Confident	Demanding
Uncertain	Bold	Arrogant
Self-deprecating	Straightforward	Overbearing
"Others' needs matter"	"Both our needs matter"	"My needs matter"

As a concrete example, imagine Sally and her husband, Jeff, have agreed that he will arrive home after work by 6 pm for dinner and that if he is going to be late for any reason he will call her to talk. How will Sally respond when three nights in one week she gets a text message from Jeff sometime after 6 pm that says, "I'm running late," and nothing more? She has options to be passive, assertive, or aggressive in her communication.

Aggressive communication says, "I matter, you don't." It is characterized by efforts to control others by dominating or bullying them through aggressive words and actions. This can mean getting big or getting loud by raising one's voice or yelling. Often, anger and pride are the emotional tools of choice for the aggressive communicator, who seeks to coerce others by making them feel small or afraid. In the animal kingdom, aggression means puffing up to full size, baring fangs or claws, and making threatening sounds. It is the grizzly bear standing on its hind legs and the low growl of the wolf from behind a curled upper lip. Aggressiveness is the fighting half of the fight-or-flight instinct. When Jeff arrives home, Sally may fly into a rage and prepare to fight: "You're such a selfish jerk! Where have you been?! You're not a real man—a real man would want to be here with me. You'd better shape up or you'll be making your own dinners from now on!"

Passive communication says, by contrast, "You matter, I don't." It is marked by efforts to control others through avoidance, submission, and self-deprecation. Passivity frequently implies a self-imposed helplessness or victim mentality that values others over self and relies on appeasement to gain acceptance or fend off hostility. The passive communicator is often apathetic or afraid, avoiding and fearing potential conflict. In the animal world, this looks like getting small, running away, rolling-over to the big dog, or standing frozen like a frightened rabbit. It's the fleeing half of fight-or-flight. In Sally's case, she might not say anything at all for fear of Jeff's reaction or of upsetting the balance in the relationship. If Jeff offers some off-hand rationalization or excuse for his behavior, Sally may meekly reply, "Oh, okay," without sharing her feelings.

Another variation of these styles is passive-aggressive behavior, which combines aggressive intent and hostility with indirect or passive action. This might include talking behind someone's back, muttering under one's breath, sulking, giving the silent treatment, or secretly sabotaging another's success. The internal message here sounds something like, "If I don't matter, then you don't either." Passive-aggressive behavior still aims to control and manipulate others, but through indirect (passive) means of aggression. The passive aggressor usually feels angry and resentful toward others about perceived wrongs but is afraid to deal with them directly, aiming instead to punish the wrong-doers by trying to stir in them feelings such as shame, guilt, embarrassment, annoyance, jealousy, or regret. Instead of confronting Jeff about his tardiness, Sally might publicly criticize him with verbal jabs among friends and family, or strike back by having cocktails most nights with a single neighbor.

As an alternative to all of the above, assertive communication consistently declares, "I matter, you matter." It honors the dignity of both parties through the use of responsible language, including *I*-statements, to reflect a consciousness of responsibility. When you are centered in *being* and connected to your authentic self, with no defense mechanisms or false masks hiding the truth of who you are, you're free to choose to express yourself confidently, directly and responsibly—in other words, assertively.

In Sally's case, she might assert, "Three times this week you arrived home late without calling me as we agreed. I get very upset when this happens because I worry about you and then I think I'm not important in your life. I also feel angry because I put a lot of energy into preparing dinners, so when I eat alone I feel I've wasted my time."

Without hidden agendas or emotional attachments to how a message will be received, our communication becomes free of attempts to manipulate, coerce, or control others, which also makes it remarkably effective. It might sound strange at first to consider assertive communication effective *because* it lacks an agenda over others. After all, you might ask, what's the point of communicating if not to achieve some desired effect or solve some problem by influencing others? Such intentions surely have their place in healthy, assertive communication. As with so many aspects of conscious living, however, what matters most is the state of consciousness from which the intentions are made.

The *having* mode of consciousness seeks to *get*, often employing manipulation through aggressive, passive, or passive-aggressive means to get what it wants or have its own way. When I communicate from this consciousness, my agenda is really about things outside myself. As we saw in Chapter 2, I may seriously compromise my authentic self by putting on a mask to get what I want or need from others. All my communication then gets filtered through a false front that's designed to *get*, whether passively or aggressively.

In a consciousness of *being*, on the other hand, the primary communication agenda is always the responsible—and often vulnerable—expression of my authentic self. Although I may make direct, straightforward statements and requests in support of creating a particular result or resolving a problem, I do so consciously, without manipulation or coercion. I choose language that reflects ownership of my emotions, wants, and needs while also respecting those of others.

Put simply, the primary responsibility of assertive communication is to assert one's authentic self in a way that respects the dignity and rights of others as well as our own. We can learn to speak about things that are unpleasant without being unpleasant. We can assert what we believe is right without needing to be right. We can disagree without being disagreeable. To communicate this way, it helps to recognize that changing or controlling others isn't our responsibility—although they may choose to change with our assertive self-expression. Our responsibility is to speak our truth as authentically as possible.

Whatever experience our relationships bring, our response is something that—with awareness and being—we can choose consciously and communicate responsibly. In choosing an assertive mode of self-expression, we increase our personal potency and interpersonal effectiveness.

The Power of Your Word

The final piece I want to share with you in this chapter about communication is the power of creating with our word. In the Bible, the Gospel of John states, "In the beginning was the Word..." Since we are created in the image and likeness of God, we also have the power to create with our word. In this section, we'll look at two ways of creating with our word based on *contracts* and *agreements*.

In the last chapter, we looked at the A→B→C of creating your experience by choosing innate qualities of your Self—your spiritual being—that you wish to embody and bring into the world. We also noted that in the Be-Do-Have paradigm of consciousness, who you choose to be does not depend on anything you currently do or have, but rather doing and having flow naturally out of your state of being. So how can we use our words to create who we want to be?

Contracts

A *contract* is a personal commitment to connect with and live the qualities of your true being that you value as important for a genuine life. To create a contract, you simply assert your Self using the power of the words, "I am…"

For example, in my family relationships I might declare, "I am a patient, loving, and kind person." I can declare this to myself and, optionally, to those around me as well. First I use my words to create who I choose to be, then I live my life connected to the qualities of patience, lovingness, and kindness, which guide my actions and help me accomplish my goals.

A contract related to career or abundance might be: "I am a competent and confident creator of wealth." In health, one might declare, "I am disciplined and dynamic," or, "I am a sexy and radiant woman." In spiritual endeavor, a helpful contract might be, "I am a devoted and trusting servant of God." In relationship, one might choose, "I am a committed, fun, and playful partner." The possibilities are limited only by your imagination.

In the interest of keeping this discussion real, I feel it's important to underscore the point that making a contract isn't delusion, pretense, or wishful thinking. It isn't just a *fake it 'til you make it* affirmation. In a consciousness of *being* lies the conviction that one's spiritual essence is innately balanced, whole, and complete and is the source of all divine qualities. *Contracting* is a commitment to bringing these innate qualities into our lives. Making a contract and creating experience is not a mechanism of denial, nor a defense against authentically handling the experiences that life presents. It's not a sophisticated method of beach-balling our emotions under a positive slogan. Remember, embracing experience with the ABCs of authenticity involves both handling and creating experience.

In handling our experience in any area of life, we can simultaneously exercise our power of choice to create the experiences we genuinely want. We can choose the specific qualities of being that we feel are most authentic (or most needed) for creating those experiences, and consciously cultivate them using the creative power of our word. By declaring our contract every day and reviewing our progress in embodying the qualities we've chosen, they come to life in us.

You will find that as your chosen qualities of being come into existence in you, they also begin to reshape your experience. As you experience life differently, new possibilities open up in your actions, behaviors, habits, and choices which previously seemed unavailable. This allows you to make solid agreements in your life with yourself and others—agreements that you are powerful enough to honor because *you are* the qualities needed to honor those agreements.

Agreements

An *agreement* is a personal commitment to specific actions, behaviors, or results that we make with others and/or ourselves as part of creating the life we want to live. Agreements are the natural consequence of a clear contract. When I am clear about who I choose to be, then I find myself making agreements to express those chosen ways of being. To make an agreement only requires declaring, "I will…"

Real relationships thrive on clear agreements that are kept. A clear agreement is one that is specific enough for me to be held accountable to it. For example: "I will pick you up at 6 pm," or, "I will publish a quarterly earnings report this year," or, "I will work out three times this week for thirty minutes" are all agreements that we can make. By contrast, unclear agreements are vague and nonspecific: "I will do it later," or, "Someday I'll get in shape," or, "We're dating."

Making and keeping agreements builds trust in relationships and promotes feelings of security, gratitude, respect, fulfillment, esteem, and confidence. Not making agreements or breaking agreements tends to erode trust and leads to experiences of hurt, resentment, disappointment, insecurity, embarrassment, and anger. Since you probably want more experiences like those that come from making and keeping clear agreements, it helps to become aware of your relationship with your word and how it affects your life. This is the foundation of personal integrity.

In everyday language, making a promise or an agreement implies that, "I give you my word." To honor my word ideally means that I keep my agreement—I do what I said I would do. In this way, my word creates not only the outcome I committed to creating but also greater trust, confidence, appreciation, and affection in the relationship. Through action, my word becomes powerful.

When you honor your word by keeping agreements, you become trustworthy in the eyes of others and of the world at large. You're recognized as someone who says what they mean and means what they say—you walk your talk. Now, when you boldly declare who you are and what you will create, the universe respects your creative power and responds by saying, "Okay!"

A fun way to build your commitment muscle in this fashion is by declaring even the simplest agreements: "I will wash this dish and put it away," or, "I will pick up milk at the store on the way home," or, "I will take you out for dinner!" Anything you create with your word by declaring it and acting on it trains both you and the universe to recognize that you're a powerful creator. Before long, you'll find yourself making bolder declarations: "I will ask that person out on a date," or, "I will increase my income by $3,000/month," or, "I will start my own business or charitable organization this year."

Once again, though, there's a good chance—if you're human!—that there will be times when you won't keep your agreements. In order to preserve the integrity of your word and of your relationships, it's important to authentically handle broken agreements just like any other experience. As soon as you're aware of a broken agreement, own it! Take responsibility for it and communicate about it assertively.

Handling broken agreements is important because failing to do so will erode trust in any relationship over time. This is true whether we believe the agreements are big or small and whether we've made them with others or with ourselves. Imagine I say to you, "I'll call you tomorrow," and then I don't call. How do you feel? Perhaps we think, "Well, it's no big deal." At some level, however, the consequences of a broken agreement—feelings of distrust, disrespect, disappointment, and resentment—are likely to manifest in your experience. Now, what happens if I do this every other day for the next week, month, or year? How will you feel then? What kind of relationship will we have?

Similarly, breaking my agreements with myself will also have negative effects. If I don't do what I tell myself I am going to do, I might think, "Well, nobody's watching. Who will know?" But the truth is, *I will know*. At some level, therefore, I am likely to experience diminished self-esteem, confidence, and trust in myself. Or, if I have the habit of internally making unclear, obligation-based agreements with myself (e.g. "I should get in shape someday") I may experience stress, guilt, or overwhelm because I haven't been sufficiently clear about what I will or won't do, and when. Creating clear agreements and letting go of self-imposed obligations can free up an enormous amount of energy in our relationship with ourselves and with other people.

Commitment

As you can see from the nature of contracts and agreements, communication that uses the power of one's word to create is powered by commitment. The power to make these commitments comes from our awareness and being—from a connection with our authentic self. We then communicate who we're committed to being and what we are committed to creating through the supportive structure of contracts or agreements.

In this way, our lives become *commitment-driven* and we draw to us what we value because of the strength of our declared commitments. No longer are we *history-driven* or *circumstance-driven*, living our lives from the outside-in. Instead, we live from the inside-out, bringing into the world what we've already aligned with on the inside. If you choose to be kind, generous, and helpful, you will agree to do things that helpful, generous, and kind people do.

Commitment-driven relationships are powerful. To establish a conscious contract with another person that says, "We are…" and to uphold that contract with agreements that say, "We will…" is a powerful way to build real relationships that work. It might be as simple as declaring, "We are committed to love and respect," and agreeing from that place that, "We will live monogamously together," or, "We will spend at least two hours each week in conscious dialogue about our relationship."

Along these same lines, wedding vows are promises that people publicly declare to one another so as to establish a foundation of commitment in a marriage. But you don't need to wait to get married, or get re-married, in order to consciously create your relationship and enjoy the benefits of commitment-driven relating. What you create in your relationships is up to you.

What are you committed to in your relationships? What have you declared is important? The more we communicate about and give our word to what we truly value, the more we create it. As we commit ourselves, through the power of our word, to embodying our values with purposeful action, we find ourselves living increasingly genuine lives.

Review

In this chapter, I've tried to share with you the foundations of empowered communication that, in my experience, best support genuine living. You discovered that the starting point of all communication is empathic listening, which directs your conscious presence with the intent to understand. You also realized the importance of applying this listening practice to yourself.

You learned that powerful and effective communication tends to be conscious, responsible, and assertive. We looked at several considerations for each of these elements, including: the fact that you're always communicating and the importance of choosing if/when/how to share; the benefits of seeking consent and sharing with *I*-statements; and the disadvantages of aggressive or passive modes of communication compared with the advantages of assertive self-expression.

Finally, we looked at communication as the power to create with your word through contracts ("I am...") and agreements ("I will...") and at how these commitment-driven approaches build real relationships and support genuine living.

In Part II, you'll have the opportunity to put these and other principles into action by taking on the ten practices presented there.

Part II: Practices

Practice makes the master.

– Don Miguel Ruiz, *The Mastery of Love*

Let's Experiment

In Part I of this book, we explored some interesting aspects of experience and used some fancy-shmancy terms like awareness, being, consciousness, vulnerability, experiencing your experience, and blah, blah, blahdy blah. So what?

That knowledge will probably mean little to you on its own. The ABCs of authenticity will have no lasting impact on your life if you never practice bringing them to your daily experience. In fact, you don't even need to read Part I before doing the ten experiments that follow because doing them is the most effective way to learn the ABCs.

That's right, I said *experiments*.

I invite you to consider these practices as experiments with experience—and to have fun with them! The great part about these practices is that you don't need to schedule a special time to do them (although you certainly could) and you can try them out whenever you want, wherever you are, using whatever you are experiencing at the time.

That said, it's important to remember that these practices are simple but not always easy. If they were easy, everyone would be doing them. But they *are* simple and any one of them is enough to change your life. For example, I took on *Step 3: Listen* as a continuous commitment years ago and it revolutionized my relationships (something I shared about in Chapter 5).

Remember, too, that developing competence with any skill or way of being takes practice, especially if it's new to you. The more you practice, the better you get, which provides further motivation and enjoyment of the process. Stick with it and reap the rewards. Practice makes the master.

Practicing the ABCs of Authenticity

Awareness	Being	Communication
1. Notice	2. Breathe	3. Listen
4. Recognize Emotions	5. Examine Your Thoughts	7. Share Responsibly
	6. Feel Your Feelings	
8. Make Distinctions	9. Play With Options	10. Create Yourself

Have I mastered these practices of authentic living? Not by far. I am deeply in process with all of them and I have humbly come to respect each one for its infinite depth, the unlimited opportunity for growth it provides. I have also come to believe that the majority of my failings in relationships can be traced to shortcomings in these practices. When resistance kicks-in and I stop practicing and experimenting, I often feel stuck and out of balance. When I return to these practices, they help me *get real* again. I begin moving once more toward balanced living and my relationships gain fresh life, flourishing in new and exciting ways.

Bringing the ABCs of authenticity consistently to my experience is the most difficult practice I know, and one I never fully achieve. But recognizing that genuine living is a practice—a lifelong practice—has helped me return to it time and again, a commitment by which my life has been immeasurably enriched.

Practice Suggestions

I've numbered these experiments in order from one to ten because they build on each other in a natural progression, and I've organized them under the ABC principle emphasized in each. To get the most benefit from your practice, I suggest following the ten steps in order at least once. This will support you in going through the A→B→C process in a straightforward way.

The simplest way to do this is to practice one experiment per day for the next ten days. Do the basic version of that practice for that day as often as you like throughout the day and just notice what happens.

Are you willing to try that?

If so, turn the page and get started! If not, I invite you to notice your resistance or aversion to practicing, and then turn the page anyway. Yes, I'm serious! You're guaranteed to learn something interesting about yourself by doing *Step 1: Notice* even just once.

Step 1: Notice

As you undertake these ten practices, you might notice your inner voice has a lot to say: "Will this make a difference? Am I doing this right? Is this helping me?" Or maybe, "What a waste of time! I've got more important things to do."

That's okay—just notice it.

In fact, that's what this first experiment is all about: just noticing. This practice is all about increasing your awareness by awakening your *inner witness*, the part of you that simply observes what's happening. In short, it's about consciously noticing your experience. Just noticing. And you can get started right away.

What are you noticing now?

Notice, too, that there's nothing to do in this experiment other than notice things. It's not necessary to judge, evaluate, label, praise, compare, make wrong, resist, or otherwise get involved with whatever you notice. Of course, if you happen to notice any one of those things happening...well, just notice *that*.

This practice is a first step in cultivating mindfulness. It will help restore your innocent perception, which is a way of looking at your experience without any preconceived ideas about it. You just innocently notice whatever you perceive, whatever is happening for you. That's it.

Noticing is extremely simple—so simple, in fact, that it might seem strange to you at first. You might hear the mind jumping in to comment on how absurd or trivial this noticing business is. Maybe it wants to turn *noticing* into some kind of complicated exercise or meditative competition that you need to do just right so you can succeed at it and become the noticing world champion, just like that one time back in grade school when you won the prize for...whoops, there it goes again! That's okay—just notice the mind likes to tell random stories.

One of the things you'll probably notice in this experiment is the mind's tendency to wander. You may find your attention going willy-nilly all over the place. So, what do you do about that? You got it—just notice.

What kinds of things might you notice? Here are some common happenings in awareness:

- *External environment*—what you see, hear, smell, touch and maybe taste

- *Body Sensations*—tingles, itches, aches, gurgles, pressure, tightness, pain, pleasure, etc.

- *What the mind is saying*—commentary, opinions, stories, and the different voices that speak

- *Thoughts and judgments*—ideas, wants, concerns, memories, *shoulds, coulds,* etc.

- *Feelings or emotions*—familiar feelings, or subtle ones, even if you can't label them

- *Language*—words, phrases, and manner of speech, internal or external (yours or another's)

- *Mood and attitude*—your overall feeling state, your outlook on life

- *Movements and actions*—your posture, the way you walk, stand, reach for a cup of tea

- *Habits and patterns*—your routines, reactions, usual ways of being or responding, etc.

Now, this practice needn't involve strain or effort. You needn't be hurried or stressed. There is no agenda, nor is there anything special that you should or shouldn't notice. Just gently tune into whatever is occurring, softly placing your attention on whatever is in your awareness at the moment, and notice it.

As you experiment with this practice, you may find it becomes quite enjoyable since there is a certain freedom in permitting yourself to be aware of what's happening without having an agenda imposed on you to do anything about it.

Actually, it can be quite liberating, fun, and comical to notice all kinds of things you've never noticed before. The experiment might unfold like an observational stand-up comedy routine, where every joke starts with, "Have you ever noticed...?"

On the other hand, maybe you'll discover this exercise upsets or frustrates you since there's so much going on in your awareness at once, or because you have some resistance to certain parts of your experience. Whatever your response to this experiment, simply notice your experience of *noticing*.

If you choose to do this exercise for a day, try to do it continuously throughout the day. Notice how well you can consciously notice. Also notice when you've gone a long period of time without noticing because you got absorbed in your experience and caught up in the drama. Then step back and notice once more. Ask yourself often, "What am I aware of now?" Finally, notice what's going on anytime you remember to practice noticing. What is happening when you become aware again of this practice?

If you like, you can also set time aside in your day to practice noticing, although it isn't necessary. (Just notice if you have a preference). Most of us have plenty of opportunities throughout the day that are perfectly suited to noticing: standing in line at the grocery store, riding the elevator, stopped at a red light, waiting on hold, in the bathroom, during commercials, and so on. Notice how many opportunities you have to practice noticing.

Notice if you practice, notice if you don't. Just try to avoid making it right or wrong. (And notice if you do!)

If this isn't the first time you've done this practice, here's a variation on it:

1A - Notice Something Specific

In this form of the practice, give your full attention to one aspect of your experience (e.g. something in your environment, like a cup or plant) and endeavor to keep your attention there, noticing what you notice about it. When you notice your attention has wandered from your point of focus, gently bring it back and continue noticing the object. After the exercise is done, notice what your attention span tends to be. Notice if it improved during the exercise, or by repeating the exercise.

Step 2: Breathe

Breath is life. The word "spirit" comes from the Latin word *spiritus*, meaning breath. In the Bible, God formed man from dust of the earth and breathed into his nostrils the breath of life; and man became a living being (Gen. 2:7). Breathing and being have always gone together. A baby gasps for its first breath of life and death follows the final exhalation. If you cease breathing for too long, you'll also cease being human!

Nature knows the importance of breathing well for our wellbeing. We naturally laugh, scream, yawn, sigh, hiccup, gasp, huff, pant, and puff in response to various situations. Performance is always tied to breathing in any activity we undertake, be it sport, music, theatre, dance, yoga, or public speaking. Relaxation techniques invariably include some breath awareness because regulating the breath can help balance our state—physically, mentally, and emotionally. Breathing calms and soothes; it also invigorates and enlivens.

Breathing is an important practice in authentic living because it anchors you in *being*. Conscious breathing connects you with your essence as a spiritual being, allowing you to bring the power of your being to your experience.

I notice that whenever I take deep, full, relaxed breaths, I'm more aware of my experience and more likely to be myself. If my breathing is shallow, tight, or uneven then there's a good chance that I'm pushing down my authentic self and holding up some kind of mask. Remembering to breathe helps. When I face challenges in life and get hit by a wave of *awareness anxiety* (see Chapter 3), then breathing into that experience helps me soothe myself and stay with it until it transforms.

Have you ever, for example, had a big cry and felt noticeably lighter after? Ever confessed a secret guilt and then felt incredibly free? Ever gotten so angry you suddenly started to laugh hysterically? Breathing into difficult experiences helps us be with them, often revealing very different experiences they had covered up. As Fritz Perls remarked, "anxiety is excitement without the breath." In their best-selling book, *Conscious Loving*,

Gay and Kathlyn Hendricks say, "Fear is frozen fun. People often get most afraid just before they are about to step out into the creative unknown, into a new possibility."

Unfortunately, we have a tendency to avoid breathing when we are anxious or when we're aware of an experience (e.g. grief, guilt, or anger) that we don't want to be with. We hold our breath to defend against it, trying to avoid or deny the experience. If instead we can *breathe into it* and *be with it*, we meet the experience with our being. Although that may prove temporarily uncomfortable or painful, it is also the healing magic by which we may come to notice something else (e.g. acceptance, peace, joy).

Breathing, like noticing, is a practice—clearly the practice of a lifetime. In this experiment, you'll incorporate conscious breathing into your daily experience and notice its effects. In a moment, I'll give you some suggestions that will help you remember to breathe, but first let's talk briefly about *how* to breathe.

Breathing helps to anchor you in *being* and connects you with the core of who you are (your authentic self) whenever it touches your *core*. I'm not talking about your core muscles, but rather your energetic core—a center of vital energy in the middle of the body (what in Taoist and traditional Chinese traditions is called the lower dantian). Located just below and behind the navel, and coinciding with your physical center of gravity, this core is a major energy reservoir that thrives on attention and stimulation. Deep, diaphragmatic breathing is a great way to activate your core.

For deep, relaxed breathing:

1. Straighten up, whether sitting, standing, or lying down.
2. Relax your shoulders, jaw, and the back of the throat.
3. Inhale slowly through your nose by drawing air down to the core, letting your belly move out and chest expand.
4. Exhale fully by letting the belly move back in and chest fall.

These are basic guidelines. It's not necessary to fret over the details. Experiment with it and notice what works for you. When all else fails, "Breathe, dammit, breathe!"

Despite that gentle encouragement, you may find you sometimes forget to breathe, especially when you need it the most. As a key component to your practice, therefore, I suggest that you *anchor* your breathing practice to some external trigger in your daily life which will remind you to breathe frequently throughout the day. Below are some suggestions—pick one that works for you.

Breathe every time:

- you check a clock
- you pick up your phone
- you open an email
- you enter a room

In order to establish your anchor for the day, practice a few times. Deliberately fire your trigger (look at a clock, or pick up your phone) and breathe deeply and freely as you do so. Repeat this three or four times so that you train yourself to do this in response to the trigger.

In addition to your one basic anchor, you can optionally spice up your breathing practice by adding one other fun anchor. For example, if in *Step 1: Notice*, you noticed something that happens frequently or loudly in your awareness, then go ahead and anchor your breathing to that trigger. Here are some more suggestions:

Breathe every time:

- you fidget or bounce
- the kids complain
- you curse or swear
- another driver does something dumb
- your partner does "that thing" they do (the thing you just can't stand!)

- you open a bill
- the dog barks
- you see or hear a certain word (e.g. "Christmas", "no", or your name)
- you notice your inner critic speaking

Remember, start with just one basic anchor and optionally one other fun anchor.

With this practice, you'll use external events to anchor your awareness about breathing, and your breathing will connect you with *being*. This way, the routine things of your day become like little *mindfulness bells* whose gentle chimes help you practice being present, supporting you in genuine living.

If this is not your first time doing this breathing experiment, I've included some variations below that you can use to deepen your practice.

2A - Breathe & Notice

Combine breathing with *noticing* (see Step 1) as part of a basic mindfulness practice. To do this, consciously put your attention on your breathing. Follow its rhythm of inhalation and exhalation, expansion and contraction. Focus your attention on the sensation of breathing. Notice the feeling of air moving across your lips or inside your nose, and the variance in temperature of air going in versus coming out. Now, every time the mind wanders away from your breath, just notice where it went and then gently bring your awareness back to breathing.

2B - Breathe & Soothe

Incorporate a soothing action along with your breathing. You might slowly and gently stroke your chest in an up-down or circular manner. Or, place one hand on your chest and the other over your core (just below the belly button) and feel them rise and fall as you inhale and exhale. Whatever you choose, it should be a simple action that you find soothing and relaxing.

Step 3: Listen

If breath is life, then in relationships understanding is air. Relationships live and breathe through a continuous exchange of understanding between people.

If I get the wind knocked out of me physically and can't breathe, then all I want is air. In that moment, everything else loses its value and meaning to me. You can offer me a banana split, a million bucks, or a ticket to Tahiti—but all I want is air. In relationships, understanding is like air. If I'm not feeling understood in a relationship then you can offer me flattery, sound advice, flawless arguments, or homemade cookies—but all I want is to be understood. I want you to listen to me and understand my experience.

Understanding cannot happen without listening. This is true in all relationships, including those with ourselves and with our higher power. I cannot understand what you want, or what I want, or what God wants, unless I listen. In Chapter 5, I quoted philosopher Paul Tillich's dictum, "The first duty of love is to listen."

So far, the first two practices of noticing and breathing have helped you develop your awareness and being, in the sense of increasing your capacity to notice and be with your experience without judging it. The practice of listening begins by directing this *conscious presence* with the intent to understand. You simply notice what someone (perhaps even you) is communicating and you endeavor to be with that person in their experience, especially their emotional experience, to such an extent that you come to understand it.

Let me clarify what I mean by "understanding." I *don't* mean an *evaluative* understanding based on judgment, which sounds like, "I understand that you are nuts; I understand this is really bad; I understand what your problem is; I understand how to fix you; I understand that you are wrong and I don't like you," and so on. That kind of understanding really isn't about the other person—it's about the listener's judgments. What I mean is an *empathic* understanding, which comes from suspending judgments and stepping fully into the other person's world. It implies peering through his unique lens of perception, feeling into his emotional experience, and assimilating the meaning it has for him.

This might sound like a tall order but I can assure you that, in listening, a little goes a long way. Since most people rarely feel heard and understood, any amount of genuinely compassionate, non-judgmental understanding usually comes as a breath of fresh air.

Maximizing your effectiveness as an empathic listener means creating a space in which others feel fully understood in their experience. Below are four general guidelines for creating such understanding through the practice of listening. Listed across from each guideline is a specific strategy that we'll discuss and that you can begin to experiment with as part of your listening practice.

General Guideline	Specific Strategy
A. Invite others to be understood	Ask open-ended questions
B. Demonstrate your desire to understand	Use good attending behavior
C. Suspend your own judgments/understanding	Avoid listening roadblocks
D. Demonstrate/confirm your understanding	Use reflection/mirroring

If this is your first time doing *Step 3: Listen,* I recommend you attempt only one of these four strategies to start with—perhaps just *3A* or *3B*. As you repeat this practice over time, you can incorporate more of the strategies into your overall listening approach.

3A - Ask Open-Ended Questions

One great way to invite others to share is to ask open-ended questions that encourage self-expression. Closed-ended questions invite only a limited answer, often just one word like yes or no. Examples of closed-ended questions include: "Did you have fun?", "Are you feeling better?", "How long did you study there?" and "Do you have any siblings?"

By contrast, open-ended questions allow the speaker to determine what's important for them to share about their experience by providing a broader invitation: "What happened for you at the party?", "What was your experience like at university?", "I'd like to know more about your family."

Here are some very broad, open-ended questions you might like to experiment with to initiate opportunities for listening with important people in your life:

- I'm here for you. What's happening in your world?
- I notice you mentioned _____. Would you like to share more about that?
- I'm curious: what's really important to you in our relationship?
- Could you help me better understand your experience with _____?
- What do you need right now?

Asking open-ended questions is just one way to invite or deepen sharing but it is often very effective. See if you can come up with at least five open-ended questions you can ask of people in your life today. Then create opportunities for them to feel understood by asking those open-ended questions and really striving to understand them when they share.

As you improve in this practice, you'll develop the ability to ask open-ended questions naturally in any conversation without having to think about them in advance. When you want to invite someone to share further, you'll naturally compose a suitable, open-ended question on the spot that encourages them to share more of their experience. Of course, over-using open-ended questions in rapid-fire succession will eventually discourage authentic sharing, so just *notice* in this experiment the right balance in asking open-ended questions.

As part of extending an invitation to hear about another's experience using an open-ended question, and especially when they begin to share, we can demonstrate our desire to understand what they have to say by how we attend to them as we listen.

3B - Use Good Attending Behavior

Imagine you are seated across from someone you are speaking to who leans back at the waist in their chair, folds their arms across their chest, makes infrequent eye contact, crosses their legs, and finally turns away from you at an angle as they reach for their phone. What are they communicating? What do you experience? Are you likely to feel understood?

In Chapter 5, we looked at how communication is always happening at some level and how non-verbal elements of our self-expression (like tone of voice, facial expressions, and body posture) comprise a large part of what we communicate overall. This is important knowledge for you as a listener if you want to consistently communicate to the other person your sincere interest in them and desire to understand them while attending to them in listening.

Attending to someone means to help meet their needs while conveying that they are valued, respected, and cared for. Just as a physician's duty is to attend to patients or a flight attendant's job is to attend to passengers on a plane, a responsible listener attends to the person who is speaking. As we have said, there is a great need in relationships for understanding. By attending to someone with your entire being—directing to them your full conscious presence—you help fulfill this basic human need for understanding.

Physically, good attending behavior means facing the other person squarely (not turned away at an angle or slouched down) in an open-body position (empty-handed, without arms folded or legs crossed), leaning forward slightly in their direction, and making comfortable eye contact. These elements can be summed up as SOLE:

S Sitting squarely
O Open-body position
L Leaning forward slightly
E Eye contact

Although there may be cultural considerations we need to be aware of and sensitive to (e.g. the amount of eye contact that is acceptable, or how close we should sit or stand to someone), overall these elements tend to convey caring and respect and to increase mutual trust in communication. They are a powerful starting point for fostering deep connection and authentic sharing. It is often said the eyes are the window to the soul, so appropriate eye contact may feel vulnerable and revealing at first but it can quickly become richly rewarding and nourishing for the soul.

Ultimately, listening is a practice of making a *soul to soul* connection with the other person by attending to them with not just the body but with our full consciousness and capacity to be present. The SOLE acronym helps remind us of the importance of making this soul-level connection, beginning with the basic elements of good attending behavior.

In your listening practice today, apply the elements of SOLE and notice their effects. Again, be sensitive to the needs of different speakers and don't overdo it by leaning in uncomfortably close or turning your eye contact into a rigid staring contest. Be conscious of their needs, but be diligent in giving them your full attention and demonstrating your desire to understand by practicing good attending behavior.

3C - Avoid Listening Roadblocks

Effective listening is a demanding practice because it requires suspending our own judgments, assumptions, reactions, and agendas in order to fully receive another person and understand them in their experience, especially their emotional experience.

If we cannot (or will not) do this, then we are likely to give a *roadblock response*. Roadblock responses get in the way of effective listening because they tend to be about ourselves rather than focused on the person speaking, including his or her need for understanding. These responses offer a kind of help that doesn't actually help, blocking the speaker from fully processing their experience and emotions.

For example, imagine yourself encountering the following workplace situation. How would you respond?

Your boss sends out an email with a critical tone and several pointed remarks to your entire team about a project that is behind schedule. The project manager replies to the email, trying to address some of the points, but the boss immediately shuts down the email exchange with a terse reply admonishing her to focus her efforts on getting the job done. Everyone in the office, including you, reads this email exchange shortly before you must attend a meeting with the project manager. On your way to the meeting, she walks up to you and says, "Can you believe that last email? He doesn't care what anyone here thinks or how hard we work. He can't treat me like that. I'll show him — I'll quit!"

Below are several possible responses you could make to your coworker. As you read each one, notice your inner reaction or gut-level feeling about it:

1. "You better watch what you say. You could get fired for talk like that, and it's not a good job market out there right now."

2. "Oh, it's no big deal. Don't worry about it. He's just stressed."

3. "You should really talk with him and clear the air. Sit down and have a heart-to-heart to get things back on track."

4. "It is as it is. You'll have to face the facts: life comes with good times and bad."

5. "Look, you *are* the project manager on this project and you *did* approve the schedule. You're always too aggressive in your forecasts. You have nobody to blame but yourself."

6. "It's probably because of your astrological chart—isn't your Boss conjunct Uranus right now?"

7. "It sounds like you're having a classic reaction against a male authority figure. Maybe he just reminds you of your father."

8. "You're a very patient and understanding person. I think you're one of the hardest workers at this company."

9. "Hey, are we going out for Chinese food after this meeting?"

10. "Just because you didn't like his emails is no reason to quit your job. That's illogical."

11. "Well, let's bring in that communications mediator that was here last year. And set up a round table to work through the issues. And implement a new review process…"

12. "You're such a whiner."

The following list characterizes the roadblock responses above: 1) warning; 2) minimizing; 3) advising; 4) philosophizing;

5) criticizing; 6) joking; 7) psychoanalyzing; 8) praising; 9) distracting; 10) logical reasoning; 11) problem-solving; 12) name-calling.

How might your coworker feel when receiving these responses? Chances are, she is unlikely to feel understood or to perceive these responses as helpful. In fact, she might experience some of them as frustrating, insulting, patronizing, condescending, manipulative, uncaring, or mean. Yet these responses represent some of the most common ways in which people offer help when faced with a situation that is emotionally-charged for the speaker.

Typically, roadblock responses carry a hidden agenda. Perhaps I'm putting up a roadblock because I need to feel superior through criticizing or name-calling. Maybe I am uncomfortable with emotions of hurt or anger and so I try to change the topic. Alternatively, I may have a need to look smart by solving a problem or feel like I'm doing a good deed by offering praise. But in each case, my response is motivated by what *I* need or want, not by a genuine desire to really hear the other person and meet their need for understanding.

Listed below are several other examples of possible roadblocks to effective listening.

Possible Roadblocks to Listening

advising • judging • moralizing
problem-solving • reasoning • arguing
warning • threatening
interrogating • probing • questioning
preaching • teaching • lecturing
ordering • directing • scolding
diverting • distracting • denying • minimizing
analyzing • interpreting • diagnosing • labeling
philosophizing • psychoanalyzing
criticizing • name-calling • blaming
sympathizing • reassuring • praising
joking • sarcasm • wise-cracking

Notice that these are all *possible* roadblocks. There are certainly healthy and appropriate places in relationships for solving problems, offering praise or advice, asking questions, providing direction, teaching lessons, using humor, and so on. As responsible listeners, however, what matters most is that we consciously choose, with full awareness, our response in any given situation. Often, the responses listed above end up as roadblocks when they are chosen unconsciously or prematurely in the listening process.

Another unfortunate consequence of roadblocks is that they tend to escalate negative emotions and hostility rather than defuse them. Just as a person who is physically suffocating will flail about in the attempt to obtain air to breathe, someone suffocating from a lack of understanding will often flail about emotionally, escalating the intensity of their message in an attempt to be understood.

Since roadblock responses deny understanding to another, that person will often dig in their heels and cling stubbornly to their experience until they feel understood in that experience. Avoiding roadblocks is a great way to offer this gift of understanding and compassion to others. Amazingly, when people feel understood in their experience they often become quite willing to let it go or change it.

In your practice today, strive to avoid listening roadblocks in your communication. As you proceed through your day, monitor yourself and just *notice* your default or habitual responses in different relationships. Try to recognize and identify your usual modes of responding and then set them aside while you continue seeking to understand the other person in their experience. If you notice the urge to respond in a manner that could be a roadblock, just *breathe* instead. Breathing will help you remain conscious and stay present in the conversation. Then, once you've heard and understood the other person, you can decide again if your initial response (whether advice, or praise, etc.) is still something you wish to share.

3D - Use Reflection/Mirroring

If our intention as a listener is to understand the speaker, then it can be helpful to actively demonstrate what we've understood from them by mirroring or reflecting back, in our own words, what was shared. Faced with the example situation given in the preceding section, one possible response to your coworker which would demonstrate understanding might be, "You're upset by how he communicated his concerns via email. You aren't feeling respected or appreciated for how hard you've worked on this project."

This kind of response represents a powerful approach to listening. First, it helps your coworker sort through her feelings and arrive at clarity about her own experience. By using your words to hold up a mirror of her experience, she gets an opportunity to see herself and the situation more clearly and to work through the problem herself. Second, she knows you have understood her and, if you haven't, she has the opportunity to correct or clarify her communication. In this way, the communication process becomes self-correcting and much more productive. Finally, your response builds trust in the relationship because you aren't trying to manipulate your coworker by immediately imposing your own agenda at the expense of her breathing the vital air of understanding.

In reflective listening, it can be helpful to mirror back both the *content* of what the speaker has said, as well as their *emotions*. This shows that we understand their emotional experience and the reasons they see for it. The following sentence fragments can often serve as helpful structures for demonstrating understanding via mirroring/reflection:

- "You feel ____ because ____."
- "When ____, you felt ____."

Here are some examples:

- *Student to Parent:* "I've got four exams next week and three shifts at work. My marks aren't great already and

I haven't even started studying. I could call in sick, but I really need the money. I'm not sure what I'm going to do."

> *Empathic Reflection:* "You feel overwhelmed and worried about your finances and your busy school and work schedule."

- *Wife to Friend:* "Paul was such a flirt at the party last night. I think he danced with four different women. It was so hurtful. Am I not good enough? Doesn't he care about me?"

    > *Empathic Reflection:* "When Paul spent all his time dancing with other women, you felt really hurt and rejected."

- *Husband to Wife:* "I've had it with that company! After all I've done for them in the past year, and they go and give the promotion to someone who hasn't been there as long as me? I really wanted that job. I would have been good at it. Bah, what's the use?"

    > *Empathic Reflection:* "You're feeling angry and disappointed because you've worked so hard and you weren't recognized for it by getting the promotion you wanted and feel you deserve."

In our application of this structure to convey the substance of understanding, certainly, we don't want to be rigid or formulaic. Accurate, empathic reflections that include both content and emotion can be made in a variety of ways. Sometimes it might be as simple as, "It didn't work out—that's painful for you." What's important here is that our response reflects an understanding of the speaker's experience, especially their emotional experience.

In your listening practice today, consciously make use of empathic reflection/mirroring in your communication. Strive to demonstrate understanding when you listen by reflecting back the speaker's experience. Experiment with this practice and discover what works. If you encounter an emotionally-charged situation and forget to use reflective listening, review it later and write down a mirroring response that could have shown more understanding. At the end of the day, write down your discoveries and lessons.

If this is an entirely new way of relating for you, then some people around you may notice this change and feel suspicious or curious. Be prepared to be honest. I suggest that you *own* your practice, share it with them authentically, and create an opening for them to be heard. For example: "I'm working to improve my listening skills. You're important to me and I want to do a better job of understanding you when you're speaking. What are you experiencing that's different in how I am listening to you today?"

Other Suggestions for Your Listening Practice

Notice, Breathe, Listen

If you experience judgments creeping in while trying to listen, simply *notice* them and *breathe*. Then go back to listening. This might be as simple as realizing you've crossed your arms and are holding your breath because you don't like what someone is saying. When you notice this, simply breathe and then return to good attending behavior (open body posture).

Combine Listening Skills

Once you've had the opportunity to try each of the skills, combine them to create a richer listening practice. For example, try asking an open-ended question then follow-up with empathic reflections. Combine good attending behavior with conscious care to avoid roadblocks. See if you can eventually incorporate all four practices into the same conversation.

Understanding is not Agreement

Many people are reluctant to really understand another person's experience or point of view because they fear doing so might imply they agree with it. Just because you listen to someone with the intent to understand doesn't mean you must agree with everything you've understood. Agreement or disagreement is an evaluative judgment which will probably just end up being a roadblock to effective listening. Understanding is not agreement. Seek to understand first and then evaluate whether you agree or disagree later, when you step back into your own world and resume making your own discernments and judgments. Separating the process of understanding from that of agreement will create great freedom for you in listening.

Step 4: Recognize Emotions

If you've been experimenting with the first three practices of noticing, breathing, and listening, then you have probably experienced a wide range of emotions in yourself and in others. In Chapter 4, we examined the anatomy of emotional experience, describing it primarily as a feeling with some thoughts attached, expressed in the body as a sensation (or physiological response):

Emotion = Feeling + Thought + Sensation

For example, the emotional state of grief consists of an overall feeling of sadness or despondency, a variety of regretful and despairing thoughts, and matching responses/sensations in the body, possibly including tears, drowsiness, a heaviness in the chest, an ache in the heart, and so on. As we practice becoming increasingly aware of these components of our emotional experience, we also increase our capacity to handle them authentically.

Emotional intelligence (often abbreviated EI or EQ) has become quite a popular term as recognition of its importance to healthy and successful living has increased in recent decades, especially in the corporate world. Such emotional intelligence begins with the capacity to accurately recognize emotions in ourselves and in others. Because the dominant aspect of emotion is a feeling (as reflected in everyday language by the commonly interchangeable use of the words *emotion* and *feeling*) emotional awareness depends greatly on identifying and describing specific feelings or affective states. To do this, it helps to have access to both extremely simple descriptive words as well as a rich vocabulary for communicating feelings.

For example, a simple starting vocabulary for describing emotions uses just the following four English rhyming words: glad, sad, mad, bad. Listed below are the kinds of emotional experiences they describe:

- glad—happy, joyful, peaceful, calm, relaxed
- sad—unhappy, gloomy, down, low
- mad—angry, enraged, furious, irritated
- bad—scared, worried, guilty, embarrassed, ashamed

These simple words cover a great deal of emotional experience in very simple terms, so they work especially well with young children. To further refine our vocabulary of emotions, we can learn to combine these four basic emotional states to describe more complex states. For example, hurt is often experienced as a mix of feeling mad and sad; depression is usually a combination of feeling sad and bad; mourning and letting go can feel like a mix of sad and glad; etc.

As we become more adept at identifying our emotions, we can learn to make further distinctions and to differentiate greater numbers of feelings, first in our awareness and then in our communication. For example, we might wish to differentiate "bad" feelings of fear from those of guilt and shame. With kids, we might also want to include sexual feelings as they mature and start to experience those natural impulses. Thus, we might grow our emotional vocabulary to the following:

glad, sad, mad, bad, sexy, or scared

From here, we may wish to further separate distinct emotional states. For example, we might distinguish surprise from fear, disgust from anger, and so on.

As this process of recognizing feelings and making emotional distinctions continues, we find ourselves developing an increasingly rich vocabulary to accurately and concretely express the incredible depth and breadth of human emotions. Very often, merely reviewing such words can be helpful in raising our emotional awareness. Listed below are words that describe common affective/feeling states, categorized by similarity, courtesy of Satvatove Institute:

The Vocabulary of Emotions

Kind, Helpful, Loving, adaptable, admired, adored, affectionate, agreeable, altruistic, amiable, amorous, appreciative, aroused, benevolent, big-hearted, brotherly, caring, charitable, cherished, comforting, compassionate, compatible, congenial, conscientious, considerate, cooperative, cordial, dedicated, dependable, devoted, diligent, empathic, fair, faithful, fond, forgiving, friendly, generous, genuine, gentle, gallant, giving, good, gracious, grateful, helpful, honest, honorable, humane, idolizing, indebted, involved, just, kind, longing, loving, mellow, merciful, mindful, nice, obliging, open, optimistic, passionate, patient, neighborly, praiseful, respectful, rewarded, sensitive, sharing, sincere, soft hearted, straightforward, sympathetic, tender, thankful, thoughtful, tolerant, treasured, trustful, unassuming, understanding, unselfish, warm hearted

Curious, Absorbed, Analyzing, attentive, concentrating, contemplating, curious, diligent, engrossed, imaginative, inquiring, inquisitive, occupied, pondering, questioning, reasoning, reflecting, searching, thoughtful

Happy, Peaceful, Accepted, amused, at ease, blissful, brilliant, calm, carefree, charmed, cheerful, clear, comfortable, complete, delighted, ecstatic, elated, enjoying, excellent, fantastic, fine, fit, full, giddy, glad, glorious, good, gratified, great, happy, inspired, joyous, jubilant, laughing, lighthearted, magnificent, marvelous, merry, optimistic, overjoyed, peaceful, pleasant, pleased, poised, proud, refreshed, rejoicing, relaxed, relieved, renewed, revived, safe, satiated, satisfied, serene, settled, smiling, soothed, splendid, sunny, superb, sweet, terrific, thrilled, tickled, tremendous, wholesome, wonderful

Playful, Joking, Witty, agreeable, amusing, breezy, clever, easygoing, frisky, frolicsome, fun loving, funny, genial, good humored, happy go lucky, hearty, hospitable, humorous, joking, jovial, mirthful, mischievous, original, lively, quick witted, smart, sociable, sparkling, spontaneous, sportive, sprightly, spry, uninhibited, vivacious

Interested, Excited, Active, alert, aroused, attracted, bubbly, bustling, busy, challenged, delighted, eager, enchanted, enthusiastic, excited, exuberant, fascinated, flustered, impatient, impressed, interested, involved, keyed up, quickened, resourceful, responsive, stimulated, tantalized, thrilled

Miserable, Troubled, Hurt, frustrated, abused, aching, afflicted, awful, badgered, battered, bothered, bruised, burdened, clumsy, crabby, cramped, cut, deprived, desolate, desperate, despair, destitute, disagreeable, dismal, displeased, dissatisfied, distressed, disturbed, divided, dreadful, futile, harassed, hassled, hemmed in, hindered, horrible, imprisoned, jammed, loaded down, lost, lousy, mistreated, oppressed, pathetic, peeved, perturbed, pitiful, poor, pressured, pulled apart, puzzled, restless, ridiculous, rotten, ruined, sore, stabbed, strained, strangled, suffering, swamped, temperamental, terrible, threatened, thwarted, tormented, trapped, tortured, uneasy, unfortunate, unhappy, unlucky, unsatisfied, unsure, upset, wiped out, wounded, wretched

Ashamed, Guilty, Embarrassed, apologetic, awkward, blamed, branded, chagrined, cheapened, condemned, contrite, degraded, denounced, disapproved of, disgraced, dishonored, disreputable, doomed, evasive, exposed, foolish, humbled, humiliated, in a bind, in trouble, judged, punished, put down, rebuked, red faced, regretful, remorseful, ridiculous, roasted, shamed, sheepish, silly, slammed, sorry, wicked, wrong

Disgusted, Suspicious, Arrogant, callous, cynical, derisive, despising, detested, disgusted, displeased, distrustful, dogmatic, doubting, envious, grudging, hesitant, indifferent, jealous, loathing, mistrustful, nauseated, nonchalant, offended, pompous, queasy, repulsed, revolted, sickened, skeptical, sneering, wary

Weak, Defeated, Shy, belittled, at the mercy of, bashful, bent, broken, cowardly, crippled, crushed, deflated, demeaned, dependent, dominated, done for, drained, drowsy, exhausted, failing, fatigued, feeble, fragile, frail, hungry, helpless, imperfect, impotent, inadequate, incapable, incompetent, ineffective, inept, inferior, insecure, insulted, intimidated, laughed at, needy, neglected, paralyzed, powerless, puny, put down, run down, scoffed at, self-conscious, shattered, small, smothered, spineless, squelched, stifled, strained, tearful, timid, tired, troubled, unable, unambitious, unfit, unsure, unqualified, unstable, unworthy, useless, vulnerable, washed up, weak, whipped, worn out, worthless

Lonely, Forgotten, Left out, abandoned, alienated, alone, betrayed, bored, cast aside, cheated, deserted, discarded, disliked, disowned, empty, excluded, forsaken, friendless, hated, hollow, homeless, homesick, ignored, isolated, jilted, lonely, lonesome, lost, neglected, ostracized, outcast, overlooked, rebuffed, rejected, scorned, secluded, shunned, slighted, snubbed, stranded, ugly, uninvited, unimportant, unwelcome

Angry, Hostile, Enraged, irritated, aggravated, aggressive, agitated, angry, annoyed, aroused, belligerent, bitter, boiling, bristling, brutal, bullying, burned, contrary, cool, cranky, critical, cross, cruel, disagreeable, displeased, enraged, ferocious, fierce, fighting, fired up, frenzied, exasperated, fretful, fuming, furious, harsh, hateful, heartless, hostile, incensed, indignant, inflamed, infuriated, irked, irritated, mad, mean, outraged, perturbed, provoked, pushy, quarrelsome, raging, raving, ready to explode, rebellious, resentful, revengeful, ruffled, sarcastic, spiteful, steamed, stern, stressed, strung out, stormy, unkind, vindictive, violent, vicious

Confused, Surprised, Astonished, aghast, amazed, appalled, astonished, astounded, awed, awe struck, baffled, bewildered, bowled over, breathless, changeable, dazed, dismayed, disorganized, distracted, doubtful, dumbfounded, emotional, forgetful, gripped, horrified, jarred, jolted, mixed up, muddled, mystified, overpowered, overwhelmed, perplexed, puzzled, rattled, ruffled, shocked, speechless, staggered, startled, struck, stunned, taken aback, torn, trapped, tricked, uncertain

Sad, Depressed, Bereaved, blue, brooding, broken hearted, dejected, demolished, despondent, destroyed, disappointed, discouraged, downcast, downhearted, dreary, drooping, dull, falling apart, forlorn, gloomy, glum, grief stricken, grieved, heavy hearted, hopeless, in the dumps, let down, lifeless, low, melancholy, moody, moping, mournful, oppressed, pained, pessimistic, serious, solemn, sorrowful, tearful, troubled, unhappy, weary, woeful, wrecked

Vigorous, Strong, Confident, able bodied, accomplished, adequate, adventurous, alive, ambitious, assertive, assured, blessed, boastful, bold, brave, capable, certain, clever, competent, competitive, confident, courageous, daring, deft, determined, dignified, dynamic, effective, efficient, encouraged, energetic, favored, fearless, firm, fit, forceful, fortunate, gifted, hardy, healthy, in control, important, independent, intelligent, keen, lion hearted, lucky, mighty, peppy, potent, prosperous, qualified, powerful, reliable, responsible, robust, secure, self-confident, self-reliant, sharp, shrewd, skillful, smart, spirited, stable, strong, sturdy, suited, sure, successful, together, tough, triumphant, victorious, vigorous, well off, well suited, wise

Afraid, Tense, Worried, agonizing, alarmed, anxious, apprehensive, boxed in, cautious, concerned, cornered, disturbed, dreading, edgy, fearful, frantic, frightened, hesitant, jittery, jumpy, panicky, petrified, nervous, numb, quaking, quivering, restless, scared, shaken, suffocated, terrified, trembling, troubled, uncomfortable, uneasy

ě

In today's practice of emotional mindfulness, you'll increase your awareness of your emotional experience and learn to recognize its component parts, including your feelings, thoughts, and sensations. But first, I want to share with you a few words of caution and encouragement. I want to emphasize that:

1. All of your emotions are valid.
2. There's nothing you need to do about your emotions in this experiment other than to observe and become aware of them.

These statements are helpful in making it safe for you to freely explore your emotional world. As we discussed in Chapter 4, many people have an emotional beach ball shoved down inside of them. Real feelings have been hidden behind false masks and façades. Thus, setting out to explore your emotional experience might feel somewhat vulnerable and threatening. Or, on the other hand, maybe it's exciting and empowering! Either way, just *notice* your emotional response to exploring your emotions as you carry on this practice throughout the day.

Also, please remember that this experiment isn't about acting on your feelings or evaluating them in any way. This exercise is just about taking a stroll through your house of awareness (see Chapter 4) to discover what emotional experience is there. It's like taking an emotional inventory. In later practices, you'll learn powerful strategies for being with the feelings you discover and examining the thoughts you find, as well as responsibly communicating them both. For now, just notice your emotions. What can you observe?

One way to begin your practice of emotional mindfulness is simply to identify your overall emotional state in the present moment. What are you feeling, primarily? What's loudest in your experience? Draw upon the vocabulary of emotions above to help you identify, as precisely as possible, what you are feeling. From there, you can explore the emotion more deeply by examining all its component parts. For example, if you start with recognizing an overall feeling (which is very common), you can then proceed to also look for the various thoughts and body sensations that accompany that feeling. What do you notice?

A second approach is to pick a physical sensation in the body (e.g. tension in the neck, or a weight on your chest) and focus on that sensation. As you focus on it, notice what thoughts and feelings arise in your awareness. What emotional message accompanies that sensation? What does it say? Listen. Attend to yourself in full consciousness, just as you did when attending to others in *Step 3: Listen*.

Finally, a third approach begins with noticing significant or recurring thoughts in your awareness and then investigating what feelings and sensations accompany those thoughts or patterns of thinking. Ask yourself, "What kind of thought is this? A happy thought? A scary thought? A sad thought?" If you consciously repeat that thought in your mind, what happens in your experience? What response do you observe in the body?

At the end of today's practice, take a few minutes to review and write down what you've discovered about your emotional world. What were your predominant emotional states during the day? What emotions do you experience most often and most easily? What patterns of thinking/feeling/sensing did you identify? Were any emotions conspicuously absent? Were there emotions missing that you would have liked to experience?

Once you've become adept at identifying the three components of your emotional experience (feelings, thoughts, and sensations), you can enhance and deepen your practice with the following variations:

4A - Breathe & Recognize Emotions

Incorporate conscious breathing into your practice of recognizing emotions. When you identify an aspect of your experience (whether a feeling, thought, or sensation), breathe into it in order to bring the full power of your being to bear. As you inhale deeply, intentionally direct the energy of the breath toward your experience in order to amplify it and make it more prominent in your awareness. Then, on the exhale, watch for other components of that experience—perhaps an associated thought or sensation in the body. Continue using inhalations to amplify what you're currently aware of and then use the exhalations to invite other elements of your experience into your awareness. What do you discover with this practice?

4B - Notice Subpersonalities & Listen

As you continue with this practice and become adept at identifying the components of your emotional experience, you may also notice broad patterns or configurations of your experience over time. As discussed in Chapter 3, these patterns of experience can often be characterized as unique subpersonalities living inside of you.

Using your breath once more to anchor you in your body and experience, begin this version of the practice by noticing the overall tone/voice/personality that is active inside of you. Breathe and invite this subpersonality fully into your awareness. I encourage you to participate in this practice of learning about your inner family of characters with a playful spirit of discovery. Ask open-ended questions such as, "Who is present now?", "What is your name?", "What do you need?", or, "What is important for you to say?" Then listen attentively with the same intent to understand as you would show to another person.

If possible, engage in an empathic dialogue with this subpersonality. Although listening to yourself this way may feel strange or unfamiliar at first, it develops meaning and depth with practice. When the dialogue is complete, or when you feel your listening capacity is fading, thank your inner visitor for his or her presence and contribution.

Whenever your inner voice is loud today, renew this practice by turning within and asking, "Who is speaking?" Then give space and listen.

Step 5: Examine Your Thoughts

In *Step 4: Recognize Emotions,* you began developing greater awareness of the feelings, thoughts, and sensations that exist in your experience. That practice, however, was only about *noticing* those elements in your awareness whereas the next two practices will equip you with practical tools for *handling* your thoughts and feelings by enabling you to be with them in conscious ways. Bringing the power of your being to the thoughts and feelings in your awareness is an incredibly powerful way of transforming them and freeing you up to create a new experience.

Socrates boldly declared, "The unexamined life is not worth living." In today's experiment, you'll learn to examine your thoughts in ways that will support you in genuine living. As we discussed in Chapter 3, merely observing the mind tends to increase one's consciousness, so examining your thoughts can be a powerful spiritual practice.

Of course, if you've never tried it before, consciously examining your thoughts might be a completely new idea to you. Listening to the voice in your head can seem like a strange step to take. As you practice, however, you'll discover it's a powerful way to free yourself from limiting beliefs and assumptions, and to connect with your authentic self.

From your earlier experiments, one of the first things you may have noticed about the mind is that most of the thoughts you experience occur unasked for. Thoughts just happen. They aren't personal. They simply appear in awareness as part of your experience. The vast majority of thoughts are involuntary, compulsive, and repetitive.

When we are identified with this stream of thinking, without examining or questioning the thoughts, we believe those thoughts are true and we personalize them. We believe we *are* our thoughts. And when this happens we frequently suffer. Without mindfulness about our thoughts they can sometimes be a lot to handle.

So how can we handle our thoughts authentically?

Rather than believing, resisting, or arguing with our thoughts, we can simply notice them as they occur and then choose to examine them more closely. When we take a step back in awareness, recognizing that we are not our thoughts, we create space in which to be with them. We can examine them with interest and meet them with understanding as the first step in freeing ourselves from them.

To create this space between our being and the thoughts in our awareness, an essential part of all the practices in this section is to *write your thoughts down*. Writing thoughts down is the key to allowing them to be carefully and consciously examined. Putting thoughts on paper puts the mind on pause, capturing a freeze frame of our thinking. Once thoughts are captured in writing it becomes a lot easier to examine them and discover how they impact our lives.

In the following sections, we'll explore a few different ways to examine your thoughts.

5A - Capture Your Thoughts

One of the most powerful ways to reveal your thoughts is to develop the habit of uncensored and unfiltered journaling or writing. This practice involves tapping into the flow of thoughts running through the mind and simply writing them down without editing or evaluating them. As you write, don't stop to analyze or judge your thoughts—just write them down. It doesn't matter if what you're thinking seems crazy, nonsensical, brilliant, random, silly, sophisticated, or anything else. Strive to write continuously for at least five minutes, or until you feel a sense of calmness and completeness from having emptied out your thoughts. Do this journaling at least twice today.

Although it can be challenging to do, one of the best times to capture thoughts is when you are experiencing strong emotions, whether positive or negative. (You may already have discovered and recorded some of these thoughts in *Step 4: Recognize Emotions*). Thoughts that accompany emotionally-charged experiences are often the loudest in our minds (indeed, sometimes they leap right out of our mouths!) and therefore the easiest to identify. It takes discipline, but writing down your thoughts when you're emotionally active can be powerfully healing and revealing.

For example, Natasha has noticed she often feels frustrated and angry with her husband, Jose, around the issue of household responsibilities. One day, the power suddenly goes out in their home after Jose has forgotten to pay the electric bill. While experiencing her frustration and outrage, Natasha immediately flips on the flashlight app of her phone, grabs a pen and paper, and starts writing. She is able to capture several thoughts, some very immediate and specific, and some more general and subtle:

- Jose didn't pay the bill! *AGAIN!*
- What an idiot!
- He's so unreliable!
- I can't count on him for anything.
- I'm so stupid—I should never have trusted him with something so important.
- I have to do everything myself.
- What will happen if we can't turn it back on today?
- I'll have to empty the fridge! All the food will go bad!
- He should be more organized.
- This should never have happened.
- The neighbors will think poorly of us.
- (I feel silly writing this.)
- Jose never does what I need him to…just like my father.
- He shouldn't let me down all the time.
- I'm always picking up the pieces in this relationship.
- I feel like I'm doing this alone, and I'm afraid of ending up alone.
- It's not safe to depend on men.
- Men are dangerous and untrustworthy.
- I really want to trust Jose.
- I feel so alone.
- Why does this keep happening?
- …

Natasha keeps writing her uncensored thoughts while the emotional charge is active. Whatever comes to mind flows out through her pen and onto the paper. After several minutes of writing, the energy dissipates and her writing stops on its own. (If you've never tried writing this way before, don't be surprised or alarmed if a *lot* of thoughts come out on paper. Keep writing as long as you can, preferably until you are emptied of thoughts, and feel calmer.)

5B - Take Inventory

Toward the end of the day, when you are feeling calm and reflective, take inventory of all the thoughts you wrote down earlier in the day. I encourage you to approach this task with a playful spirit of discovery and a genuine desire to learn about yourself. If you were truly uncensored in your writing, there are likely to be some things on the page that may seem challenging, shocking, or even hilarious to you now. Other thoughts might seem confused, absurd, or embarrassing. Your inner critic or judge might have something to say about them, or about you!

Thus, if at any point the process of inventorying your thoughts triggers you emotionally, simply start writing out your new thoughts. Journal your thoughts about reviewing your thoughts until you once more feel calm and emptied out.

Now, with full consciousness, begin to review your thoughts and be with them. Give them as much acceptance as you can. What do you notice as you take inventory of these thoughts?

For example, you might wish to circle in the same color pen all the thoughts associated with a certain feeling. Perhaps in red you will circle all the angry thoughts. In another color, circle all the fearful thoughts. Put stars next to the loudest thoughts. Underline repeated or recurring thoughts.

What do you notice? What patterns emerge? What area of your life do your thoughts focus on the most? What things do you tell yourself repeatedly? How many thoughts express a form of judgment? How many argue with reality? What was this experience like for you? Remember: *write down your answers.*

5C - Inquire into the Thoughts

Having taken inventory, you are now ready to inquire into the thoughts you have captured on paper. These thoughts have become frozen in time and cannot escape, so you can safely begin to examine the truth of them. You can begin to separate fact from fiction and identify which thoughts support you and which ones don't.

To inquire into a thought, you will simply ask some questions about it. Question the thought. Here are some sample questions you might like to ask:

1. What feelings arise when I believe this thought?
2. What bodily sensations/responses occur when I believe this thought?
3. Who, in me, was speaking this thought?
4. Do I really believe this thought?
5. Do I want to continue believing this thought?
6. What am I getting out of this thought?
7. Is this thought serving me?
8. Could I see this thought as just a thought?
9. If it were just a thought, what would happen?
10. ...

There are many possible questions you can ask of your thoughts in order to free yourself from them. One very popular and powerful process of inquiry to investigate thoughts is presented in *The Work* of Byron Katie. In her approach, you write down your thoughts and judgments about someone and then ask yourself a series of four questions about each one before turning the thought around. The questions are:

1. Is it true?
2. Can you absolutely know that it's true?
3. How do you react when you believe that thought?
4. Who would you be without the thought?

These questions can be powerful aids in bringing a compassionate understanding to our thoughts. Rather than wrestling with our thoughts to get free of them, only to end up further entangled with them, we inquire into them and find we are released. As Byron Katie describes it, "I don't let go of my thoughts—I meet them with understanding. Then *they* let go of me."

Today, make a practice of capturing your thoughts on paper (or use thoughts you've recently captured) and then inquire into them using the questions provided above. For maximum benefit, jot down your answers after you ask each question.

Step 6: Feel Your Feelings

If you've been diligently practicing the first five steps, then you've probably come across some pretty strong feelings at certain points. In Chapter 4, we described feelings as the dominant element of emotional experience, which includes *feelings*, *thoughts*, and *sensations*.

Now, I don't mean to imply that any of these elements of experience is more or less important than the others. However, we tend to think of emotions as mostly being about feelings. Also, for any given feeling, there can be many similar thoughts or sensations that go with that feeling. For example, when feeling angry we can have many different angry thoughts and bodily responses. Typically, certain kinds of thoughts and sensations just seem to pop up whenever a particular feeling arises. To better understand the importance of feelings, consider the following analogy.

Have you ever gone to a fair or carnival and played the Whack-A-Mole game? In this game, little plastic moles pop their heads up out of holes in a machine and the player's job is to use a rubber mallet to whack each mole on its head and send it back down into its hole. This is easy at first but as the game speeds up it becomes nearly impossible to whack all the moles. In a similar fashion, we often end up hammering away in vain at the thoughts or sensations in our experience, playing a losing game by ignoring the feeling(s) out of which they arise. Authentically dealing with a major feeling can be like reaching around and unplugging the game—suddenly those thoughts and sensations don't pop up in awareness anymore.

In today's practice, you'll experiment with consciously feeling your feelings. This is important because, for most of us, feeling our feelings is a daunting prospect—it's vulnerable and scary. Most of us have repressed our feelings for so long (remember the *emotional beach ball* from Chapter 4) that accessing them even a little can bring up the fear that they will come rushing up and knock us over. We fear that by letting our feelings out, even a little, the dam will burst and we'll be swept away in a rush of strong emotions coming to the surface.

At the same time, however, it's impossible to be fully authentic and to discover our deepest truths without fully experiencing our feelings. Often, feelings must be keenly felt and experienced before they can be released or transcended, thereby creating a space for a new experience. In their best-selling book *Conscious Loving*, Gay and Kathlyn Hendricks list this willingness to feel all your feelings as "Fundamental Requirement #1" for creating conscious, co-committed relationships. Similarly, author John Gray's first published book is entitled, *What You Feel You Can Heal*. Whether in our relationship with ourselves or with others, feelings have a key role to play. In many ways, feelings are the royal road of experience in authentic relationships.

Remember to Breathe

When allowing and accepting feelings into your awareness, it helps to be anchored in being. Recall from Chapter 4 that authentically handling your experiences in the house of awareness requires *being with* them. As you learned in *Step 2: Breathe*, deep diaphragmatic breathing is a great way to help you stay anchored in being and connected with your authentic self. As you take on today's practice of feeling your feelings, remember to breathe. Breathe deeply. Breathe often.

6A - Feelings about Feelings

One of the most common blocks to feeling our feelings is that we have negative feelings about our feelings. Strange as it sounds, these *meta-feelings* occur frequently when we are wearing masks or holding up the façade of a false self. With any false self, certain feelings will be forbidden. Thus, your false self will often use other feelings to block the forbidden ones.

For example, you start to feel angry and then right away you feel guilty about that anger. Or maybe you experience desire as a stirring of sexual energy and then you feel ashamed about your sexual feelings. Perhaps you begin to feel sad, only to end up feeling angry about the weakness that crying could imply for you. You might even feel excitement or joy and then feel nervous or anxious about whether that joyful feeling is safe to have, or if it will last.

In order to deepen your ability to feel your feelings, it helps to first accept how you feel about having feelings. Although that might sound a bit like going in circles, it's a very powerful way to create greater freedom to feel. Often, this amounts to dropping a mask (or part of it) in order to see what's really going on inside—it begins to peel away the outer layers masking your authentic self.

To explore your feelings about having feelings, set aside a few minutes at different points today and repeat this series of steps during those times:

1. Ask: "How do I feel now?"
2. Ask: "How do I feel about that feeling?"
3. Say: "I accept these feelings of _____ and _____ in me."

Remember to breathe as you do this. You can repeat these steps until you feel a sense of completion for the current round of practice. Throughout the day, you can return to this practice in your awareness even without setting aside a specific time. At the end of the day, review what you discovered in this practice. Which feelings are the most difficult for you to feel? Which meta-feelings occur most frequently? Write down your discoveries.

6B - Let Them Flow & Let Them Go

Challenging, chronic, negative emotions can often be the most significant obstacle to living the life we truly want. Personally, I've experienced periods of recurring negative feelings at multiple points in my life. Over the years, I have found that when I resist those feelings, they often persist, patiently waiting for me to hear the message they are carrying. However, when I can allow those feelings to flow in my experience and be with them compassionately, I am better able to hear their message and let them go.

Letting feelings flow and letting them go is the natural course that emotional energy wants to run. Animals clearly display this natural processing of emotional energy. For example, whenever our family dog gets excited and barks defensively at something she hears outside, she begins releasing that energy as soon as she knows everything is okay by shaking her head and body, huffing, and stretching. Usually, she's asleep on the floor again within minutes. In a similar way, the deer or rabbit that escapes its predator trembles for a few moments to let the fear pass through the body before returning to grazing. Illustrating the same principle, author and spiritual teacher Eckhart Tolle gives the example of two ducks who have an altercation in a pond. Very quickly after their encounter, they separate, flap their wings to disperse the energy from the body, and return to a peaceful state.

When we interfere with feelings running their natural course like this, they get stuck inside us and become problematic. In Chapter 4, we looked at a variety of defense mechanisms and coping strategies that are commonly used to avoid our natural flow of feelings. When we *beach-ball* our emotions and push them down through these means, they cannot run their natural course. We may not even realize that we're spending all our energy managing the beach ball instead of living our lives.

So how can we learn to feel our feelings? How can we let them flow and let them go?

Although there are many helpful techniques and methods available for getting in touch with feelings, all of them depend greatly on your own courage and willingness to accept your feelings and to release them. This brings up the principle that structure is no substitute for substance. In this practice, the substance is feeling your feelings fully and surrendering them, and it is primary. The structure (method, technique, or approach) you use to assist you in that practice is secondary.

That being said, having some structure usually helps to get started in this practice because very few of us were ever given any training in how to feel our feelings, or had good role models from whom to learn. One ultra-simple structure I have found enormously useful for getting in touch with emotional experience, especially feelings, works as follows:

1. Go to a quiet, safe place where you will not be disturbed for at least 20 minutes.
2. Lie down or sit comfortably so you can breathe deeply and easily.
3. Begin deep, slow, and rhythmic diaphragmatic breathing. Keep this breathing going throughout the exercise.
4. Tune into your self-awareness and speak out loud the following sentence, filling in the blank with whatever you currently notice in your experience:
"I am experiencing ____."
5. Continue breathing and completing that sentence out loud with whatever you are experiencing in the moment.

In this practice, you may initially find yourself only saying that you're experiencing certain bodily sensations ("I am experiencing an itch on my nose") or various thoughts in your mind ("I am experiencing thinking about what I need to do today"). As you continue breathing and speaking, however, the practice will take you deeper into your experience and various feelings will naturally surface in your awareness. You can then speak directly about your feelings: "I am experiencing feeling anxious about..."; "I am experiencing frustration with..."; "I am experiencing wanting to..."; "I am experiencing sadness"; and so on.

The key in this process is to keep it going continuously and to keep the sentences short. Don't pause to think about or analyze your experience, and don't elaborate into a long-winded story in an attempt to explain it. This exercise is direct and repetitive. Use the lead-in phrase and speak your experience as accurately and authentically as you can in simple and straightforward language. Once you feel complete with the process for the time being, continue breathing deeply and being with your experience in silence for several more minutes until you feel ready to end your session.

Other Techniques for Letting Go

There are numerous other structures you can use to assist you in moving deeper into letting your feelings flow and letting them go. Popular among these currently are the different forms of Emotional Freedom Techniques, as well as the many variations on releasing, or letting go, techniques. Excellent introductions to the latter can be found in Dr. Patricia Harrington's book, *Releasing: The New Behavioral Science Method for Dealing with Pressure Situations*, and Dr. David R. Hawkins' book, *Letting Go: The Pathway of Surrender*.

Once you've experimented with the structure offered above, you might wish to explore these or other methods to discover which suits you best in releasing your emotions. Remember, however, that structure is no substitute for substance – the key to unlocking all of these techniques is your willingness to allow each feeling to be fully experienced and then surrendered, so that it runs its natural course and is released.

Step 7: Share Responsibly

In previous steps, you've made great strides in the A→B→C practice of handling your experience authentically. You have learned to become more aware (A) of your emotional experience and to be with (B) the thoughts and feelings in your awareness in conscious ways. Now you are empowered to make choices about what parts of your experience you want to communicate (C) to others.

Sometimes, once you've responsibly handled a thought or feeling there's nothing left of it that needs to be shared with others. On the other hand, there are many times when responsibly and vulnerably sharing your experience is the most authentic option and helps to create connection and closeness in a relationship.

In Chapter 5, we explored different aspects of responsible and assertive communication. In this section, you'll practice taking full *ownership* of your experience and sharing it responsibly using assertive communication.

How to WIN in Relationships

One of my favorite strategies for cultivating assertive communication appears in Dr. David Wolf's book *Relationships That Work: The Power of Conscious Living*, where he describes the WIN acronym:

W what happened
I inside thoughts & feelings
N needs & wants

This is a three-part structure for guiding assertive communication that separates external events and facts from internal interpretations or reactions. Using the WIN formula helps limit the number of assumptions, judgments, accusations, and other counter-productive elements in the communicated message.

For example, imagine Tomas has agreed with his wife, Sarah, that he will pick up the kids from the dentist the next afternoon, but he doesn't show up. Instead, Sarah gets a call from the dentist informing her the kids need to be picked up because the office is closing soon, so she drops what she's doing and drives over to pick them up.

In a mode of passivity, Sarah might not say anything about this to Tomas out of fear of upsetting or angering him, or to avoid tension in the relationship. In a mode of aggressiveness, Sarah might attack and berate Tomas, yelling at him and hurling insults about his inadequacy as a husband or father. Or, she might choose an assertive mode of communication and employ the WIN strategy.

In the first step about *what happened*, we simply state the facts as we understand them. Thus, Sarah might say, "We agreed yesterday that you would pick the kids up from the dentist at 5 pm. I got a call from their office at 5:15 saying you weren't there and they were closing. I left my staff meeting to drive over and get the kids." In making this observation, Sarah is sharing her perception of what happened on the outside. She is giving an honest account of what she believes to be externally true based on her experience.

Notice what Sarah is *not* doing in this step. She isn't exclaiming, "You don't care!" or, "You're a terrible father!" In stating the facts, we strive to report them cleanly and accurately without *-izing* about them—that is, without emotionalizing, moralizing, dramatizing, analyzing, rationalizing, politicizing, demonizing, infantilizing, patronizing, and so on. We simply state the facts to the best of our understanding.

In the *inside thoughts & feelings* stage, we take ownership of our inner experience and share it responsibly and respectfully. This generally means using *I*-statements to reflect this consciousness of ownership, both for our experience and our self-expression. In Sarah's case, she might say, "I feel hurt and disrespected by this, and I am angry with you. I also feel anxious when you're missing because I worry about what might have happened."

Notice how Sarah's stance of responsibility and use of *I*-statements leaves her empowered in her experience. She isn't using *You*-statements to blame ("You make me so angry!"), which would put the power of her feelings in Tomas's hands. Nor is she accusing or wrong-making ("You shouldn't be so disrespectful and thoughtless!"), which is likely to trigger defensiveness and emotional reactivity in Tomas. Rather, she is owning her ability to respond, including choosing anger. She is cleanly and clearly asserting the truth of her inner experience.

Having expressed her understanding of *what happened* (W) and her *inside thoughts & feelings* (I), Sarah may wish to pause and create space for Tomas to respond. If he chooses to do so, she can practice listening empathically, suspending her judgments and directing her conscious presence toward him with the intent to understand. She can use good attending behavior, avoid listening roadblocks, and demonstrate her empathic understanding of what he says through active or reflective listening (see *Step 3: Listen*).

At an appropriate point in the conversation, Sarah also expresses her *needs & wants* (N), once more taking full ownership of them with responsible language and *I*-statements. For example, Sarah might say to Tomas, "I'm really needing to feel respected and cared for right now. I want our relationship to be one of harmony and cooperation. For that to happen, I need you to honor our agreements, or to communicate with me in advance if you won't."

In making these statements, Sarah's priority isn't to get her way or make herself right through either passive or aggressive means of manipulating Tomas. Such motives would reflect a consciousness of *having*, based on *getting*. Instead, she intends to create—from a consciousness of *being* authentic, vulnerable, and assertive—a relationship of integrity based on mutual respect. She trusts that cultivating an atmosphere of understanding and empathy is the best way for everyone's needs to be met and their desires fulfilled.

This last step of *needs & wants* is vital in the process. If we omit this step, then our attempt at responsible and assertive communication may sound like we are blaming our inside thoughts and feelings on what happened, since that is all we have shared. More commonly, though, the difficult feelings or thoughts we experience in a challenging or conflict situation arise because one or more of our needs aren't being met, or our values are being violated. By including the last step, we take ownership of our needs and desires and communicate them assertively. Doing so lets the other person know what we value and what we want to create with them, making a positive, productive, and satisfying outcome much more likely.

Does using the WIN strategy guarantee a satisfying and productive outcome? No, it does not. It is only a guiding structure to support the substance of Sarah's authenticity, responsibility, and assertiveness in her communication. The truth is, no communication can *guarantee* a constructive response. However, Sarah's conscious use of the WIN strategy, in showing respect for Tomas (without threatening, attacking, or blaming him), will maximize the chances that he will choose to accept the invitation to also express himself responsibly and so engage in meaningful dialogue about the issue.

For today's experiment, practice being authentic and assertive using the WIN strategy to create at least three meaningful communication experiences. Bring a spirit of discovery as well as an open mind and open heart to the process. What will you discover? At the end of the day, write down your observations and experiences about these conversations. What did you notice? How did you feel? What experiences did you handle or create?

Step 8: Make Distinctions

In Chapter 3, we discussed awareness as the basis for consciousness. As your awareness grows, you become more conscious and increase your capacity to recognize and distinguish different aspects of your experience. For example, in *Step 4: Recognize Emotions*, you practiced raising your awareness of the components of emotional experience, learning to distinguish specific feelings, thoughts, and sensations. You also began to expand your vocabulary of emotions to precisely identify different affective states.

To make a distinction means to recognize and understand the distinctive nature or character of something. For our purposes, we're mainly interested in making distinctions about human experience and spiritual reality. Making such distinctions is a vital part of genuine living and the A→B→C process for authentically handling experience. Without an accurate awareness of what's happening for us—what's *real*—we simply cannot handle it effectively.

Most of us learn to appreciate the importance of making distinctions based on our earliest experiences of handling physical reality. For example, to navigate our three-dimensional world, it's useful to be able to distinguish spatial dimensions, discriminate between solid objects and empty space, recognize distinct shapes and colors, gauge distance, understand the effects of gravity, and so on. Correctly distinguishing, through our sense perceptions, these aspects of physical reality, is enormously helpful for navigating the world effectively.

Just imagine, say, riding a bike. How well could you ride a bike if you couldn't make the distinctions above? Would it even be possible? Before you correctly distinguished the subtle experience of balancing on a bike, you couldn't ride. However, once you distinguished that experience adequately, you were cruising around the block. You were effective!

Similarly, in navigating the reality of relationships, it's useful to be able to make distinctions about emotional experience. Even at a young age, we start learning to discriminate between different non-verbal expressions of emotion, such as tone of voice or facial expression. Although we also quickly learn that boys and girls have gender differences that are important to be aware of, most of us are never helped to further distinguish the key emotional differences that men and women typically exhibit in terms of how they think and feel.

When two people with complementary (masculine and feminine) sexual essences try to relate without understanding their emotional differences, it's a bit like trying to ride a tandem bike blindfolded and dizzy—not very effective! It would also be terribly comical, if it weren't so tragically painful. Lacking an awareness of even the simplest distinctions, it sometimes feels like the so-called opposite sex is simply incomprehensible. We're so alien to one another that it seems we must come from different planets—a sentiment popularized by John Gray's bestselling book *Men are from Mars, Woman are from Venus*.

Making distinctions is important when dealing with any reality, be it physical, emotional, social, financial, or spiritual. Anything that impairs our capacity to accurately recognize the reality we're dealing with also limits our ability to handle that reality effectively. Like it or not, as human beings we have a number of these limitations, or impairments. Chief among them is the limit of our conscious awareness. Many spiritual texts and teachers tell us that the primary human shortcoming is simply ignorance. Our basic conundrum is that the mind is unable to distinguish truth from falsehood, reality from illusion (*maya* in Eastern traditions; or *mitote* in popularized Toltec wisdom).

The highest truth is reality distinguished from illusion for the welfare of all.

– Śrīmad-Bhāgavatam (Vedic spiritual text)

Without awareness we cannot accurately recognize the nature of whatever reality we are dealing with, so we struggle to deal with it effectively. The motivation of education and learning, then, is usually to raise our awareness and help us make better distinctions about a given topic we wish to understand and work with effectively. Life is not black and white, so making increasingly sophisticated distinctions about it means learning to *embrace the gray*. In relationships, making even minor emotional and communication distinctions can produce major results.

Suddenly, in making a new distinction, we see things differently and find ourselves miraculously opening up to new possibilities of being and behaving. For example, understanding the ABCs of authenticity is already an important distinction that empowers you to handle your experience more effectively. You've probably also picked up several other important distinctions while reading this book. In your first practice for this section, we'll review some of those distinctions together.

8A - Review and Apply Important Distinctions

This practice is straightforward: at least three times today, review one or more of the key distinctions you've learned in *Get Real: The ABCs of Authenticity*. As you do, be sure to identify how each one currently applies to your life. If you like, you can flip through the book and look for sections that really spoke loudly to you. What stands out? What's clearer upon reviewing? And, most importantly, how is it relevant and applicable to you now? Alternatively, read on and we'll review a few distinctions together.

A key distinction we made early on had to do with your identity. We made the distinction that we are all *spiritual beings* having a temporary human experience, not human beings having the occasional spiritual experience. Thus, we distinguished our spiritual nature from our material nature (which includes the mind and body). We said that acknowledging our spiritual nature is very important for making sense of life and discovering new ways of being. How does this distinction sit with you? What do you feel about it?

One communication distinction you learned is that *understanding is not agreement*. Thus, you can listen empathically to another person with the intent to understand without the fear that your understanding implies agreement. You're free to agree or disagree later, based on a full and complete understanding of what the other person has said. This distinction is enormously liberating and helps you navigate the reality of relationships more effectively, since everyone has a basic need to feel understood. In what relationships are you currently resisting understanding the other person because you don't want them to think you agree? In which of your relationships are you avoiding listening because you fear perhaps you *will* agree once you see things from the other person's perspective?

Another distinction we made is that *structure is no substitute for substance*. In *Step 6: Feel Your Feelings*, you learned a simple structure (breathing and saying, "I am experiencing ____") for helping you get in touch with what you are experiencing inside. But we distinguished this structure from the substance of the process, which is really the willingness to connect with your authentic self and to feel the feelings that are there inside of you. Similarly, you have learned several helpful communication structures (e.g. SOLE, WIN, *I*-statements, reflective listening), none of which are substitutes for the substance of genuine empathy, understanding, responsibility, and assertiveness which they are meant to assist in cultivating and conveying.

Where in your life are you using structure without substance? Are you just going through the motions, cut off from any emotion? Have you taken on these experiments with a genuine spirit of discovery and full participation? Are you (mis)using newly acquired structures to continue to hide behind a more subtle, sophisticated mask? Are you (ab)using structures as an excuse to feel superior to others or to give yourself license to communicate irresponsibly?

We also made some distinctions having to do with emotions. For example, you learned that *emotions have a message*. As messengers from your inner world, emotions can have a natural and healthy place in your life. To elaborate on this, consider that the following emotions can be natural, healthy, and appropriate to certain experiences in our lives:

- Guilt can be a guide to conscience.
- Grief or sadness is appropriate to mourning.
- Fear can warn us of imminent danger.
- Anger can be appropriate to setting firm boundaries.
- Pride in one's actual accomplishments can support healthy self-esteem.

These naturally occurring emotions are really only *negative* when we repress or resist them, turning them into chronic experiences that adversely affect our health, happiness, and the life we want to live.

I may, for example, need to learn to differentiate the natural pride that comes from feeling satisfaction in a job well done from an ego-inflated, prideful sense of superiority over others that I hold up as a mask. Similarly, if someone I care about passes away, then sadness, tears, and mourning this loss may be a healthy and appropriate response for some period of time. However, if several years later I'm still consistently sad, depressed, and refusing to move on with my life, this may be a pattern of emotionality that I need to look at responsibly and own. Am I dealing authentically with my emotions, or indulging in emotionality? Am I perpetuating these feelings for some perceived benefit or payoff? Am I secretly choosing them all the while protesting, "I don't want this"? Where am I really coming from with this life situation?

In relationships, we are faced with similar questions of discernment all the time: Where am I coming from in this relationship? What am I needing or wanting to express in this conversation? Do I need to speak up about something, or work it out on my own and let it go? How can I be boldly assertive without seeming aggressive? Where is the dividing line between quiet patience and unhealthy passivity? How can I state my needs without sounding needy?

What situations are you thinking of in your life as you read these questions? What distinctions have you learned to make that you can now apply to your life? Write down your answers. This practice is just about raising your awareness of the distinctions you are starting to make. You don't have to figure them all out today—making distinctions is a lifelong practice.

Making distinctions is also a vital part of genuine living. By connecting with our authentic self, we get in touch with the reality of our experience and learn to deal with *that*, rather than trying to deal with something else which we've manufactured out of false masks and illusions. Dealing with reality, as distinguished from illusion, is always empowering. Coupled with a stance of one hundred percent personal responsibility, we can consciously choose how to respond (via our *response-ability*) to whatever reality we are currently facing. When we powerfully handle our past, we are then free to consciously create something new in the present.

8B - Distinguish the Past: Victim vs. Responsible Stories

In this practice, you'll make a few more powerful distinctions, apply them to your past, and then experiment with reclaiming a position of responsible empowerment in your life.

In the early chapters of this book, we looked at what I call the *vulnerability problem*, acknowledging that human life is innately vulnerable. There is so much we cannot control and, the fact is, painful experiences can and do happen in life. Moreover, each of us starts out life in an extended period of enforced and excruciating vulnerability. In this state of vulnerability, we feel even more exposed to our experience and more influenced by it.

Yet we also made the distinction that vulnerability is not victimhood. Being vulnerable is part of being human. Indeed, we can learn to embrace our vulnerability to create closeness and connection through communication. We can learn to accept our humanity and empower our real freedom through responsibility, by choosing how we will respond on the inside to what happens on the outside. From this standpoint of personal responsibility, being a victim is a choice—just one possible response we can choose.

I believe it is important to make a distinction here between being *victimized* and being a *victim*. Most of us have had external experiences of being wronged, mistreated, taken advantage of, or otherwise victimized in the world. You may have had your car stolen or home burglarized, fallen prey to financial scams or deceptions, or even been emotionally, physically or sexually assaulted or abused. In our society, what the other person did was wrong, both legally and morally. The pain of such victimization is very real. Naturally, you are likely to experience strong emotions as part of moving past the experience, emotions that might include hurt, anger, or fear.

Acknowledging and living through such experiences of *victimization*, however, is different from becoming a *victim*, which implies a lingering inner attitude of bitterness, resentment, blaming, and giving power away to past transgressors. In short, being a *victim* means making others responsible for your life now. It means buying into a story about the past that renders you powerless today.

Such story-telling is a powerful practice. Each of us has a story. What is the story of your life?

The stories you tell about your past profoundly influence the present and determine your future. A story, though, is really just a bundle of thoughts. In *Step 5: Examine Your Thoughts*, you learned how to capture your thoughts on paper and inquire into them. In this exercise, you'll do something similar with respect to a victim story about a past experience and transform it using distinctions of responsibility. (Because this is a form of examining your thoughts, it's once again imperative that you *write down* your story on paper in order to freeze-frame your thoughts.)

To begin, select an experience of victimization from your past, preferably one that still holds some emotional charge for you. Perhaps it was a time you felt wronged, hurt, or mistreated. It might be something you are carrying a resentment or grudge about, related to a specific incident or person(s). It might be a time when you felt unfairly taken advantage of. When you have a specific and concrete experience in mind, follow the steps below.

1. Your Victim Story

The first version of your story is your victim story. Include in this version all the ways you were wronged, your judgments about the people involved (or God), where you place blame or fault, who was wrong or bad and why, what should or shouldn't have happened instead, and how you feel about it. Describe this experience in full detail and get absorbed in the process of telling this story. Write the story so as to convince other people that you were (and still are!) a *victim*.

2. Your Responsible Story

The second story is your responsible account of the same incident. In this version, write the story as the author and creator of your life, taking full responsibility for your experience. Drop your masks. Be honest and authentic. Bring full awareness and being into your communication (A→B→C). Stick to the facts or use responsible *I*-statements that take ownership of your feelings and perceptions. Disclose any pertinent information you may have omitted from your victim story about this incident. Clearly separate events (what happened) from the meanings, interpretations, and conclusions you drew about them (your inside thoughts and feelings).

Even if you don't yet believe this responsible version, commit to writing the story with full participation and conviction from a standpoint of one hundred percent personal responsibility. Write this story so as to convince the reader that you have taken complete ownership of the experience and are fully responsible for it *now*.

3. Review your stories

Read over both versions of your story and try each one on for size. How does it feel? What emotions arise as you review each story? Which one works for you? Which story empowers and supports you best? Which bundle of thoughts is more authentic? Also consider: what consciousness is reflected in the language of the story? Can you identify any masks in your victim story that you removed when telling the responsible story?

For the next 24 hours, I invite you to adopt and experiment with the perspective created in your responsible story. Color your consciousness with this viewpoint of one hundred percent responsibility and look at your experience through that lens. How does this impact your life?

Additionally, I invite you to share both versions of your story with someone you trust. Ask them for input about how they feel when listening to each one. Which story is more compelling and authentic in their eyes? What's their honest feedback? (You might want to invite them to share using open-ended questions and then use your listening skills to hear what they have to say).

As you increase your ability to make distinctions, including between past events (external) and the meanings and interpretations you gave to them (internal), you'll gain a newfound freedom. No longer will past experiences hold power over you because you can now handle them authentically in the present. You are empowered to re-evaluate if they still mean what you thought they did when you were young, vulnerable, and less experienced. Do your conclusions and beliefs still make sense given what you know now? Often they do not, and you can remake the meanings you made, stepping out of the limitations of the past into a new realm of possibility. Although you cannot change the past, from a standpoint of authenticity and responsibility you can change what it means, and so explore what options are available to you now. You can learn to choose and play with those options, recreating anew who you want to be and how you choose to live.

Step 9: Play with Options

One of the most rewarding aspects of handling your experience authentically is that you immediately create an opening to possibility, a space for something new. You give yourself options.

Let's say that you become aware of a pattern of emotionalized behavior in your life that is part of a mask that you hold up to the world. You recognize this pattern isn't authentic for you. It doesn't support the life you want to live. The moment you can see it, you begin to be free of it, to disentangle yourself from it and create a space in which to choose something new.

For example, I had a pattern of reacting defensively and angrily anytime I felt challenged, confronted, or criticized. It was part of a defense mechanism designed to defend the *Mr. Know It All* mask that I shared about in Chapter 2. The first time I really saw this pattern was after a tiring day of conflict at work where I believed I had won several arguments and defended (rather angrily, I would now say) my ideas against the input from several other staff members. Experiencing that I "knew it all" that day, I was feeling quite good about my (false) self. Because I was so identified with my mask at the time, when the mask was validated *I* felt validated. In relaying the day's events to my girlfriend that evening, I got so caught up in telling the story that the following words came tumbling right out: "It really feels good to win that argument. I knew I was right...and *I love to be right!!*"

We were both stunned. We paused, blinked, and then burst out laughing that I had spoken so candidly. Apparently my usual inner filters had switched off and *Mr. Know It All* was speaking uncensored. In that moment of lucid insanity, I was able to see how much of my life had been run by a mask that needed to be right and to defend itself against being wrong. With that awareness came a whole range of new possibilities that I had never considered before, and I was free to begin playing with options.

I played with options of waiting before responding, asking for clarification first, or stepping away from unproductive discussions. I played with my imagination, envisioning myself getting worked up and agitated to the point of absurdity—wild-eyed and frothing at the mouth—then decided whether that was the direction I really wanted to go. Eventually, I started playing with the option of *agreeing* with the criticisms I received: "Hey, that's a good point!" Of course, playing with options didn't mean I never again experienced the pattern of reactivity or got triggered by challenge or criticism. I still did, but it happened much less often, and when it did occur the new awareness I held around it afforded me many more options with which to play.

To this day, I can still get triggered by really aggressive confrontation or what I perceive as attack, but rarely does this trigger lead to a reactive behavior that I later regret. Usually, there's a lot of other options on the table. There is a space now between the stimulus and the response—a space of being.

In today's practice, you'll first identify something in your life that isn't aligned with what you genuinely value and want for yourself. Then, you'll cultivate a space of being by playing with different options for responding to that situation.

To begin, choose a habit, a pattern of behavior, or a persistent way of being that you're aware of which isn't supporting you in living the life you want to live. It might be related to the food you eat, your exercise habits, an unhealthy dynamic in a significant relationship, something you're procrastinating on, a pattern of emotional reactivity, or something else you've uncovered in your house of awareness.

Next, simply notice that pattern. Hold it in your awareness for examination separate from your self. Just have a look. What do you see? (If this starts to make you uneasy, remember to *breathe* and then return to *noticing*). How would you describe this pattern to someone else? Do you recognize it as one of the defense mechanisms or coping strategies discussed in Chapter 4? What's the trigger for this experience? What activates it? What are your usual choices and actions that enable this pattern to continue?

You don't need to evaluate or criticize yourself about what you observe. For now, this is just like *Step 1: Notice*. If you find you are being critical of yourself or wind up experiencing anxiety, just notice that. You can even pop briefly into a practice from *Step 6: Feel Your Feelings* to handle your emotions as they come up. Again, remember to breathe.

Once you've handled any immediate experience and are centered again in a space of just noticing things, begin to experiment and play with possible options.

The whole idea of playing with options is to try on new ways of being in a playful way. It's not about rigidly changing once and for all, but rather about stepping out of your past, with its conditioning and programs about how you *should* be, and stepping into the possibility of new and different ways of being—just for now, just to try, just for a change. Then, if you like that experience better, perhaps you'll choose that option again sometime.

This ability to play with options is an important part of the A→B→C process of *creating experience* that we outlined in Chapter 2. Following the ABCs, you become aware (A) of a quality that you value, you consciously choose to be (B) that quality, and you communicate (C) powerfully as that quality in your words, actions, and choices. In today's experiment, you'll play with options that will help open you to new ways of being.

So what options are available to you? I invite you to consider and play with the following options:

Get Curious

One option you might want to play with is becoming curious about this experience in your life. Instead of being judgmental, critical, or ashamed of what you are dealing with, you could play with getting really curious about it. What would curiosity look like when directed toward yourself? How would you embody a playful spirit of discovery and sense of adventure? Picture yourself in full curiosity mode. How do you look? Can you endeavor to find one good thing in your life that has come about because of your experiences with this challenge? What are the silver linings? Taking it a step further, ask yourself, "As a spiritual being having a human experience, how come I might have chosen to have this experience?"

Say, "Thank You for Sharing"

If the voice in your head is relentlessly telling you unhelpful or unsupportive things, play around with acknowledging it instead of resisting it. Tell your inner speaker, "That's very interesting—thank you for sharing!" or, "That's a unique perspective you've got there—thank you for sharing!" Normally, when you shine a light on a negative inner voice, it tends to get quiet. For some reason, it only likes to speak from the shadows. So when you hear it, acknowledge it and thank it for sharing.

You can also take ownership of your inner protector/controller by complimenting it for doing its job: "Of course you're trying to keep me safe, small, and the same—that's your job, isn't it? Great work! Your message has been received—thank you for sharing!"

Exaggerate the Experience

Another option is to exaggerate the experience you are having, either in your mind or (if safe and responsible to do so) in your actual behavior, until it becomes comical and absurd.

For example, occasionally when either my partner or I are feeling frustrated or disappointed because our personal desires have been thwarted by the demands of life, we will sometimes playfully act out our displeasure in a greatly exaggerated, full-blown childish display. We cross our arms across our chest, stamp one foot, make the biggest frown possible, huff out loud, and protest in a petulant tone, "No! I don't wanna ____!" Frequently, exaggerating our resistance this way helps dissolve it.

Alternatively, if you find yourself routinely swallowing your anger and having trouble speaking up, you can exaggerate this tendency until it becomes absurd. Hold your breath and don't let it go. Puff out your cheeks. Widen your eyes and look in the mirror. Picture steam coming out your ears and a whistle blowing.

If acting out the exaggeration wouldn't be safe or respectful, then you can use your imagination to picture the exaggerated scenario. For example, I would picture myself rabid, wild-eyed, and frothing at the mouth when I was triggered with anger. I would see myself turning into a kind of werewolf and snarling, howling, or barking at people. I'd make a little movie in my head—a theatre of the absurd. Suddenly, I'd be laughing instead of feeling angry.

Out Yourself

Sometimes, just admitting, acknowledging, or confessing to another person what's happening for you is therapeutic and breaks the spell of whatever is keeping you stuck in an old pattern. Play with this option of calling out what's happening for you. Out yourself. Doing so immediately helps you shift by taking ownership of the experience. This is part of the A→B→C process for handling experience authentically by sharing responsibly. For example:

1. "I feel sad, like tears are just below the surface and need to come out. I'm dizzy and nauseous. I wonder if I start crying if I'll ever be able to stop."

2. "I'm terrified. Like a dear in the headlights. I feel paralyzed by indecision and uncertainty. Like I can't even speak."

3. "Wow, I'm really a thundercloud of a bad mood right now, aren't I? I'm Mr. Stormy Pants. By Thor's Hammer, I'm surely in a bad mood!"

4. "I'm doing it again, aren't I? I'm doing the quiet, sulking thing because I'm feeling hurt about something."

Rephrase Responsibly

Often, self-limiting or self-defeating talk sounds very black and white. There's little room to argue with beliefs which declare that things *are* such-and-such. When posing as absolutes, limiting beliefs project themselves out of the past, through the present, and into the future, making them seem like they have been true for all of time and always will be.

One option for stepping out of the limitations of the past is to rephrase these thoughts with responsible language which introduces choice and puts a limit on the belief instead. Consider the following examples of rephrasing "I can't" language around specific behaviors:

1. "I can't tell my spouse what I feel."
   - → "I choose not to tell my spouse what I feel."
   - → "Until now, I have chosen not to tell my spouse how I feel."

2. "I can't ask for a raise."
   - → "For whatever reasons, I am choosing not to ask for a raise."
   - → "Until now, I have chosen not to ask for a raise."

The first rephrase introduces the power of choice. The second limits the belief to the past, instead of limiting *you*.

When our beliefs are really judgments about ourselves or others, we can play with rephrasing those responsibly, too. For example:

3. "I'm not important."
   - → "Apparently, I choose to see myself as unimportant."
   - → "Until now, I have chosen to experience being unimportant."

4. "Men can't be trusted."
   → "For some reason, I choose to view men as untrustworthy."
      → "Until now, I have chosen to distrust men."

These are just a few of many options available to you. As you practice playing with these and other options, you create a space in your experience for something new, something different. You strengthen your ability to step out of the past and to consciously create yourself and your life—and that brings us to the final practice.

Step 10: Create Yourself

Communication creates. It is powerful. Whatever you are communicating consistently in your life is likely to become your experience eventually. When we consciously choose what to communicate we are powerful and deliberate creators. When what we communicate is aligned with what we truly value, then we are living genuine lives.

In Part I of this book, we introduced the A→B→C process for creating experience as follows:

Aware of what I value in my Self → Being those qualities → Communicating my Self powerfully

Centered in a consciousness of being, we can embrace the innate qualities of our spiritual being and cultivate them in our character. In the Be-Do-Have paradigm we discussed in Chapter 3, there is nothing we need to *do* or *have* in order to *be* a certain way. Cultivating qualities that are innately ours is an inside job that doesn't depend on externals. All that's needed is for us to *own* these qualities of our true Self by choosing them and affirming them in our life.

Thus, in order to experience, say, kindness in my life, I can choose to be a kind person. I cultivate kindness in my character by committing to being a channel for that quality in the world. In this way, I surround myself with kindness by embodying it. I *am* it. I experience fulfillment by fulfilling my potential to become that which I most desire and yearn to experience.

One very powerful way to create ourselves is by declaring our choices through conscious communication, using the power of our word. In Chapter 5, we touched briefly on the supporting structures of *contracts* ("I am…") and *agreements* ("I will…") to assist with our self-creation. In the experiments in this final step, you'll practice creating yourself by establishing a personal contract to embody qualities that you value, along with clear agreements that will help you express through purposeful action who you've chosen to be.

Notice the order of creation here in a Be-Do-Have paradigm. First, we create a contract with ourselves, declaring, "I am _____." Then we create an agreement based in action, declaring, "I will_____." In this way, who we choose to be guides what we will do. Inspired, purposeful action naturally flows from a consciousness centered in being. When I have committed to being a kind and loving person, then I take actions that support the expression of that loving kindness—not to prove who I am, but as the natural expression of who I know myself to be.

When you practice making commitments through contracts and agreements, your life becomes purpose- and commitment-driven. Living on purpose through commitment is powerful, and it creates incredibly rich and rewarding relationships. The power to create and communicate genuine commitments comes from fully embracing your awareness and being—that is, from being in touch with your authentic self.

A vital aspect of being authentic with respect to our commitments requires double-checking that they are truly what we want for ourselves. For example, when establishing agreements or aspiring to new goals, it is important to ask: Is this commitment really mine? Do I *own* it? Or is it someone else's goal or vision that I have taken on, perhaps to gain their admiration or approval? What do I really want? As you proceed with today's practice, keep checking-in with yourself about whether what you are creating is authentic for you.

10A - Create a Contract: *"I am..."*

To begin this practice, identify an area of your life in which you would like to experience greater fulfillment, enjoyment, and satisfaction. It might be in a specific relationship, with your family, in your career, your community, finances, living situation, recreation, education, or some other area.

As a first step, rate your current level of fulfillment in this area of your life on a scale of zero to ten (0—10), with zero being no fulfillment whatsoever and ten representing complete fulfillment. What is your rating?

Now ask yourself, who would you like to be in this area of your life? How would you like to show up? What experiences would you like to create for yourself? What would it look like for you to be living a ten in this dimension? Go ahead and creatively envision what that is. When you're clear about what it looks and feels like, ask yourself, what qualities of your spiritual Self would be fundamental for you to connect with and embody in order to experience a ten in this area of your life?

In Chapter 4, we explored the power of being and reviewed a list of one hundred virtues as a starting point for identifying specific qualities you might want to call upon in your being. You may wish to flip back and review that list of possibilities as a starting point. Alternatively, complete the following sentences to help you identify which qualities are essential for you in this life area:

- I am committed to being…
- What's important to me is…
- Something I really value in my Self is…
- What I want most is to be…
- This part of my life is all about…
- Above all else, I choose to be…

Once you've identified the spiritual qualities you want to embody and bring into your experience, create a contract to declare who you are as those qualities, beginning with the words, "I am…" The following are examples of possible contracts for different life areas:

1. "I am bold, confident, and unstoppable!" [career]
2. "I am a passionate and playful spouse and lover." [relationship]
3. "I am an honest, reliable, and trustworthy man." [family]
4. "I am vibrant, alive, and full of life!" [health]
5. "I am firm, fair, and flexible." [parent]
6. "I am a determined and disciplined learner." [education]
7. "I am a devoted and faithful servant of God." [spiritual]

8. "I am a joyful, relaxed, and positive person." [recreation]
9. "I am an inspiring, engaging, and responsible leader." [community]

Once you have created your contract, practice declaring it to yourself. How does it feel? Is it convincing when you say it? Does it sound authentic? At first, it may feel unfamiliar and awkward to you, especially if you are choosing qualities that represent growth opportunities for you. Stick with it. Declare your contract in your mind and especially out loud. Claim these qualities of your spiritual being. Review your contract throughout the day and speak it aloud as many times as possible. How does this impact your experience?

There is a saying that *what you focus on expands*. Often, simply focusing your awareness on the qualities in your contract will bring them into being. Communicating your contract to yourself (and to others, if you choose) is a powerful way to expand who you are in conscious ways.

10B - Make Agreements: *"I will…"*

An important part of creating with your word is giving your word to form agreements that support you in genuine living. Having committed to embodying certain qualities through your contract, you're now ready to commit to specific actions and outcomes which are aligned with those ways of being and the results you want to create in your life. Agreement is based in the language of "I will…" and sounds like:

- I agree to…
- I promise that…
- You can count on me to…
- I commit to the following actions…
- Before <specific date>, I will have…

In my experience, all relationships operate by agreement. This is true whether it is your relationship with yourself or with other people. The only question is whether those agreements are unconscious, unclear, and uncommunicated, or whether they are clear, conscious, and communicated. When we make clear agreements and honor them, we strengthen our creative power, build trust in our relationships, and cultivate feelings of self-esteem, respect, gratitude, and confidence.

You can begin to strengthen your commitment muscle in any relationship by declaring and honoring simple agreements. This is pretty straightforward—just make promises and keep them! "Honey, today I will make dinner for us at 5 o'clock." Or, "I will have that report on your desk by 9 am tomorrow." Remember, a clear agreement is specific and concrete, something to which we can be held accountable.

To supercharge your experience of communicating your agreements, combine them with a declaration of what you value and who you are committed to being (as identified in your contract). For example:

1. "I am committed to being trustworthy and dependable in this relationship. This week, you can count on me to be home by 6 pm for dinner every night. Also, I will fix the fence on Sunday."

2. "What's important to me is that you know I care about you and respect you. I commit to never again use name-calling when we have a disagreement. I will always speak to you with the care and respect you deserve."

3. "I value our friendship and want us to be honest with each other. I will no longer hide things from you or evade your requests. From now on, when you ask me a question I promise to give you a straight answer."

4. "I'm committed to being helpful and supportive. I will be available to you Saturday from 3 pm to 8 pm, no interruptions, to help you with ____."

5. "What I want is for us to work harmoniously together in a spirit of cooperation. When there are important decisions to be made, especially financial decisions, I promise to always consult you first before taking any action."

In your practice today, experiment with declaring what you're committed to creating in your character and in your relationships. Share with others what's really important to you and communicate clearly to them what actions you're agreeing to take as part of your commitment.

Seize this opportunity to create yourself through communication. Have fun with it! Be bold, be courageous, be adventurous! Step out of your habitual ways of being and embrace new possibilities.

10C - Handle Broken Agreements

For your word to remain powerful and creative it is essential that you honor your word. Honoring your word is the foundation of integrity in relationships, which builds trust and ultimately makes things work! Ideally, *honoring* your word means *keeping* your word. That is, you keep your agreements. You follow-through reliably and do what you said you would do. You're known as a man or woman of your word; a person of integrity.

That said, if you're really leaning into your commitments and living a purpose-driven life fueled by powerful agreements and inspiring goals, then chances are there will be times when you don't keep your word. When living a genuine life, you'll naturally give your word to many things that are important to you and, despite your best efforts, you'll end up breaking some of those agreements on occasion.

Part of living from one hundred percent responsibility is choosing how you will respond when you realize you won't keep an agreement, or when you've already broken one. As soon as this happens, I suggest it is helpful to immediately *honor* your word by communicating with the people who are (or will be) affected by you not *keeping* your word. This preserves or restores your integrity.

If you know in advance you won't honor an agreement, for whatever reason, you can use the ABCs to handle that situation authentically with the people who will be affected. Perhaps it means you re-negotiate the agreement and then recommit. Or, maybe you find an alternate arrangement that can be agreed upon. Communicating proactively this way conveys a great deal of care and respect for the other people, and there is a good chance they will be willing to renegotiate the agreement when you share honestly about what constraints or challenges you're facing.

When you realize you already have a broken agreement, I suggest it's also best to handle it right away. Now, this doesn't mean making excuses or inventing a good story about why you haven't kept your word. From a committed standpoint of one hundred percent responsibility, the only valid explanation is that you've made certain choices in your life that have created this outcome. Being accountable to those choices is an authentic way of handling the situation.

My favorite strategy to use in handling broken agreements is called *the five A's*, described below. This strategy sandwiches an honest account of why the agreement was broken, between other elements that are helpful in restoring a relationship to full integrity and interpersonal connection. Here are the five A's:

1. Acknowledge
2. Accept
3. Account
4. Apologize
5. Amend

Let's walk through these steps to see what's involved.

The first step is to *acknowledge* that I have broken an agreement, and that this probably has an impact on the person(s) with whom I've not kept my word. Implicit in this step is to understand, with full empathy, the hurt, anger, confusion, and loss of trust the other(s) may be feeling.

The second step is to *accept* responsibility for the broken agreement and the impact it has. From a standpoint of one hundred percent personal response-ability, I responded (or failed to respond) in a certain way that led to me not honoring my word. Taking ownership of that outcome sidesteps any victim-oriented blame or helplessness.

In the third step, I give an honest *account* of the choices I made (or didn't make) that directly or indirectly contributed to what happened. This does not involve story-telling, excuse-making, or defending myself. It means humbly and honestly accounting for my choices. Because I'm not hiding behind façades or masks here, this step often isn't very flattering, but rather vulnerably reveals my humanity to another. On occasion, I might actually have made very good choices and still not met my agreement, and I can be equally honest about what actions I took without dramatizing the challenges or circumstances I faced.

Having acknowledged the broken agreement and its impact, accepted responsibility for it, and accounted for the choices related to it, the fourth step is to *apologize*. Notice that this isn't the first step. Spoken prematurely and without context, apologizing for a broken agreement can sound empty or hollow, and it may be more about my need to save face than about genuinely expressing regret to the other person. The apology, however, is included here because—spoken at the right time and in the right way—the words "I'm sorry" can be miraculous in restoring the soundness and workability of a relationship.

In the fifth step, I make *amends* by declaring what I am committed to doing to set things right. Often this means following through on the agreement at a later time. It might, however, require additional actions to get things back on track. In consultation with those affected, while ensuring I take full ownership of the amends process, I create and communicate a course of action that will address the impact and the original agreement (if it's still relevant).

To use the five A's effectively, it also helps if you don't confuse integrity with morality. This is a vital distinction. You see, it's neither right or wrong, nor good or bad, if you break an agreement. The fact is, it just doesn't work in relationships. Just as a bridge or a building with compromised integrity won't work or perform as it should, a lack of integrity in relationships also means they won't perform—they won't work. So handling your broken agreements isn't about dealing with morality—it doesn't make you bad or wrong—it's simply about restoring integrity so that the relationship(s) can continue to work.

Although you may feel "bad" (guilty, ashamed, disappointed, and so on) when you don't keep your word, these feelings are just more of the impact that you can take responsible ownership of. You can handle the feelings authentically in your awareness with the power of your being, and even communicate them if necessary as part of the process. But be careful that you don't wallow in guilt, or angrily attack and berate yourself as a way of pre-empting and deflecting the anger you might fear in others. Often, we unconsciously think, "If I show I'm angry enough at myself, then others will feel sorry for me and won't express *their* anger." This kind of emotional manipulation game only puts you further out of integrity, assuming you're committed to being authentic and honest with the person(s) involved.

In your practice today, use the five A's to restore your integrity for any broken agreements you become aware of. If you're already aware of broken agreements, even from the distant past, that you never cleaned up, this is a great opportunity to get complete with your past and free up new energy and vitality that has been drained by your awareness of having been out of integrity. You'll be amazed at what cleaning up your relationships this way will create. In relationships, cleanliness is indeed next to Godliness.

How do you get to Carnegie Hall?

Practice, practice, practice!

Additional Suggestions

Now that you've been through all ten practices, you'll have a pretty good idea of which ones appeal most to you. The ones that you enjoy are great practices to continue with at this time. There will also be some practices that are growth opportunities for you. These are useful to return to and experiment with periodically. You may also wish to create some *practice pairs*—for example, taking one practice that you really enjoy and combining it with one that is more challenging for you. See if you can create hybrid practices that are effective and powerful for you. For example, conscious breathing is a practice that's easily combined with any of the others.

Another great way to deepen your practice is to buddy up with a friend. Make a clear agreement to take on a practice for a period of time and then share openly and authentically with one another about your experience with that practice. Compare notes. Celebrate successes. Support and encourage each other. This communication will reinforce your learning and also give you more opportunities to practice being authentic (i.e. to be vulnerable, to share responsibly, to listen, to honor agreements, and so much more).

Finally, you might want to repeat these ten experiments over a longer period of time, focusing on one practice per week for, say, ten weeks. How might your life change in a few months if you practiced consistently over that period of time? I invite you to try it as an experiment and find out!

Farewell

I hope this finds you enlivened and excited about the principles and practices in this book and the new possibilities that await you now. Whether you are reading this farewell message after experimenting for the past ten days, ten weeks, or ten years, I am confident that the ABCs of authenticity can remain a lasting source of new realizations and growth opportunities for the rest of your life—or, for at least as long as you're still on the road to enlightenment!

Genuine living is a practice—the practice of a lifetime. It's a commitment to continually discovering your authentic self, creating real relationships, and living in alignment with what you hold most dear. I want to honor you for your commitment to this process and I encourage you to carry on confidently with your journey. Practice putting the ABCs to work every day and see how they continue to transform your life and relationships.

Being authentic, being *you*, is a marvelous gift to offer—one that nobody else can give. Just being *real* is already a generous service to the world. When you're authentic about your experience, it serves. When you connect deeply and vulnerably with others, it serves. When you consciously direct your awareness, being, and communication to cultivate empathy, understanding, and compassion, it serves.

I hope you will give of your authentic self, in a spirit of service, using what you have learned in this book. Surely that won't always prove easy, so I leave you with these words of encouragement:

*The best way to find yourself is to
lose yourself in the service of others.*

– Mahatma Gandhi

Acknowledgments

Praise be to Thee, O Lord, for the gift of our existence, and the opportunity in this fleeting life to rediscover that which is eternally Real. All Glory be to Thee.

To Karen, Mackenzie, and Carson—my greatest teachers of what's *real*. I am grateful for the privilege these past years of being welcomed into your lives. Thank you for being the love that you are, and for sharing so much of that love with me.

I would also like to express my thanks for the spirit and service of Dr. David Wolf, the founder of Satvatove Institute, whose work is the source of so many of the practical tools and principles of communication that are inextricably woven into the fabric of my life and of this book. Truly, you bring goodness to the world.

To my friends and brothers: Wayne Steinke, for a second lease on life; Mark Anielski, for the model of all things genuine in what I do; and Michael Haynes, for love. I am grateful for the many other dear friends and teachers, especially those women of remarkable character, who have supported me over the years.

I am deeply indebted to Bhadra Reid, for her patience, generosity, and skill in editing; to Lisa Browning for her guidance and expertise in getting the book published; and to those who offered their input and personal experience of reading the manuscript, especially Dr. Joy van Kleef and Dan van der Wolf.

And last, but not least, thanks to my father—for grit.

Bibliography

Anielski, Mark. *The Economics of Happiness: Building Genuine Wealth.* Gabriola Island, British Columbia: New Society Publishers, 2007.

Bennett, Hal Zina. *The Lens of Perception.* Berkeley, California: Ten Speed Press, 1987.

Brown, Brené. *The Gifts of Imperfection.* Center City, Minnesota: Hazelden, 2010.

Brown, Brené. TEDx Talk: *Brown, Brené: The Power of Vulnerability.* Jun 2010. Retrieved online: http://www.ted.com/talks/brene_brown_on_vulnerability

Carson, Rick. *Taming Your Gremlin (Revised Edition): A Surprisingly Simple Method for Getting Out of Your Own Way.* New York: HarperCollins Publishers, 2003.

Covey, Stephen R. *The 7 Habits of Highly Effective People: Powerful Lessons in Personal Change.* New York: Simon & Schuster, 1989.

Fiset, J. *Reframe Your Blame: How to Be Personally Accountable.* Calgary, Alberta: Personal Best Publications, 2007.

Frankl, Victor E. *Man's Search For Meaning.* New York: Washington Square Press, 1963.

Goleman, Daniel. *Emotional Intelligence.* New York: Bantam Books, 1995.

Gray, John. *Men are from Mars, Women are from Venus.* New York: HarperCollins, 1992.

Gray, John. *What You Feel You Can Heal: A Guide for Enriching Relationships*. Mill Valley, California: Heart Pub., 1984.

Harrington, Patricia. *Releasing: The New Behavioral Science Method for Dealing with Pressure Situations*. New York: William Morrow and Company, Inc., 1984.

Hawkins, David R. *Power Vs. Force: The Hidden Determinants of Human Behavior*. Carlsbad, California: Hay House, Inc., 1995.

Hawkins, David R. *Letting Go: The Pathway of Surrender*. Carlsbad, California: Hay House, Inc., 2012.

Hendricks, Gay and Kathlyn. *Conscious Loving: The Journey to Co-Commitment*. New York: Bantam Books, 1990.

Hendrix, Harville. *Getting the Love You Want: A Guide For Couples*. New York: Henry Holt and Company, LLC., 1998.

Mate, Gabor. *Hold On To Your Kids: Why Parents Need to Matter More Than Peers*. Toronto: Random House, 2004.

Napier, Augustus and Whitaker, Carl. *The Family Crucible: The Intense Experience of Family Therapy*. New York: Harper & Row, 1978.

Popov, Linda Kavelin. *The Virtues Project™ Educator's Guide: Simple Ways to Create a Culture of Character*. Austin, Texas: Pro-Ed Inc., 2007.

Prochaska, J. O., Norcross, J. C., Diclemente, C. C. *Changing for Good*. New York: HarperCollins, 1994.

O'Connor, Elizabeth. *Our Many Selves: A Handbook for Self-Discovery*. New York: Harper & Row Publishers, 1971.

Rogers, Carl R. *On Becoming A Person: A Therapist's View of Psychotherapy.* New York: Houghton Mifflin Company, 1961.

Stefaniak, Jerome. *Intimacy in Action: Relationships That Feed the Soul.* Houston, Texas: Inner Awakenings, 2000.

Stone, Hal and Sidra. *Embracing Our Selves: The Voice Dialogue Manual.* Novato, California: Nataraj Publishing, 1989.

Tolle, Eckhart. *A New Earth: Awakening To Your Life's Purpose.* New York: Penguin Books, 2005.

Wolf, David. *Relationships That Work: The Power of Conscious Living.* San Rafael, California: Mandala Publishing, 2008.

Yalom, Irvin D. *Love's Executioner: And Other Tales of Psychotherapy.* New York: Basic Books, 1989.

Index

A

ABCs, 21, 25, 106
    alignment of, 30
    interconnected, 32
act, 9, See masks
aggressiveness, 92
agreements, 97, 175
    broken, 98, 180
    renegotiating, 181
    the five A's, 181
anxiety, 53, 81
    as excitement, 113
assertiveness, 91, 153
attachment, 11
attending behavior, 120
authentic self, 14
    communicating, 95
authenticity
    ABCs of, 21
    as alignment, 34, 78
    as gift, 31, 187
    as work in progress, 29
    reward for, 167

awareness, 37
    happenings in, 110
    house of, 60
    practices, 106

B

babies, 23
beach ball, 63, 136, 150
Be-Do-Have, 43
being, 55
    being with, 56
    practices, 106
    quality of, 28, 56, 69
breathing, 113
    to anchor being, 114
Brown, Brené, 12

C

choice, 34
commitment, 99, 176
communication, 77
    agenda, 94

aggressive, 92
assertive, 91
breakdowns, 84
choice in, 79
conscious, 85
consent, 86
empowered, 77
mulligans, 91
non-verbals, 78
passive, 93
practices, 106
self-correcting, 126
conflict, 51
    inner, 51, 54
    outer, 52
congruence, 30
connection, 5
consciousness, 37
    levels of, 39
    paradigms of, 41
    reflecting language, 44
contracts, 95, 175
conversation, 79
coping strategies, 65
courage, 13, 83
Covey, Stephen R., 38
curiosity, 169

D

dantian, 114
Dass, Ram, 52
declaration, 175
defence mechanisms, 63, 81
disconnection, 7
discovery, 4, 60, 81, 144, 156, 169
distinctions, 157
distracting, 65
Do-Have-Be, 42

E

elephants, 60
emotional intelligence, 131
emotions, 57, 131
    anatomy of, 57, 131
    as message, 59
    beach ball, 63
    vocabulary of, 133
empathy, 77, 81, 117
empowerment, 18
enlightenment, 16, 187

experience, 3
    creating, 18, 27, 169
    embracing, 18
    emotional, 57
    exaggerating, 170
    experiencing of, 17, 56
    experiments with, 105
    handling, 18, 26
    inquiring into, 31
    mirroring, 126
    ownership of, 56, 60, 153
    recurring, 18
    resisting, 16, 62
    unexperienced, 18, 61

F

façade, 9
false self, 9, 167
feelings, 131, 147
    letting go, 150
    meta-feelings, 148
Franklin, Benjamin, 69
free will, 68

G

genuine living, x, 13, 19, 35, 175, 187
get real, 4, 6, 21
good own-ya!, 73
Gray, John, 148, 158

H

handling emotions, 141
Harrington, Patricia, 152
Have-Do-Be, 41
Hawkins, David R., 69, 152
Hendricks, Gay and Kathlyn, 114, 148
Hendrix, Harville, 5
honoring your word, 98
house of awareness, 60
human
    being, 14, 43, 159
    condition, 15
    spirit, vii, 15, 55

I

identity, 10, 159
    authentic, 14
impairments, 158
incongruence, 31
inner
    alarms, 54
    animal, 84
    personalities, 49
    voice, 46, 109, 170
integrity, 183
I-statements, 87

J

journaling, 142
Jung, Carl, 9

K

Katie, Byron, 145
keeping your word, 180
know thyself, 85
Krishnamurti, Jiddu, 84

L

language, 44
    of emotions, 133
    rephrasing, 172
lens of perception, 118
limitations, 15, 158
listening, 80
    empathic, 81
    guidelines, 118
    reflective, 126
    roadblocks, 124
    strategies, 118
    to self, 83
    to understand, 84

M

masks, 9
    downside of, 10
    identification with, 167
    in communication, 77
    of feelings, 149
mastery, 105
Maté, Gabor, 11
McGraw, Phil, 63

mindfulness, 47, 109
    bells, 116
    emotional, 136
mirroring, 126
morality, 183
Mr. Know It All, 24, 51, 167

N

noticing, 109
numbing, 66

O

options, 167
oranges, xi
out yourself, 171
own everything, 73
ownership, 56, 69
    avoidance of, 64

P

passive-aggressive, 93
passivity, 92
perception, 37
lens of, 37, 81

performance, 113
Perls, Fritz, 113
persona, 9, 53
playing with options, 167
power
    of being, 67, 70
    of choice, 34
    of your word, 95
    to make commitments, 99
practice, x, 32, 105, 106
    opportunities, 111
    suggestions, 106, 185
presence, 117
principles, x, 4
progress not perfection, 29
projecting, 63
purpose, 176

Q

quality, 28, 69, 175
questions, 31, 72
    open-ended, 119

R

realm of spirit, 14
reflection, 126
relationships
    agreements in, 97
    as vehicle, 53, 71
    being in, 70
    commitment-driven, 100
    communication in, 85
    helping, 30
    real, ix
repression, 63
responsibility, 56, 68
    100%, 73, 74, 180
    owning, 74
    story, 164
roadblocks, 122
    to understanding, 125
Rogers, Carl, 30
roles, 10
Rowan, John, 49

S

Self, 15, 19
self-concept, 10, 4
self-expression, 7, 77
responsible, 85
self-identity, 47
self-talk, 46
separation, 6
service, 187
sex, 44
sharing
    choices in, 86
    inviting with questions, 119
    irresponsible, 90
    responsible, 85, 153
shoulds, 62
    as agreements, 99
    vs. options, 169
skeletons, 60
soothing, 116
spirit, 113
spiritual being, 14
spiritual growth, 16
Stone, Hal and Sidra, 11, 50
story, 162
    responsible, 164
    victim, 164
stuck, 19
subpersonalities, 49, 51, 138
substance vs. structure, 150, 156, 160
substitutes, 66

survival, 8
   strategies, 8, 47, 54

T

Teilhard de Chardin, Pierre, 15
therapy
   Imago, 5
thoughts, 141
   being with, 141
   capturing, 142
   inquiring into, 145
   stream of, 46
Tillich, Paul, 80, 117
Tolle, Eckhart, 150
triumph, 67
trust, 98

U

understanding, 72, 117
   as air, 117
   as purpose of listening, 84
   empathic, 31, 80, 117
   evaluative, 117
   for love, 84
   suffocating from lack of, 125
   vs. agreement, 129, 159

V

validation, 167
victim, 34
   story, 164
virtues, 69, 177
voices, 46
   acknowledging, 170
   listening to, 141
vulnerability, 7, 54
   hangover, 13
   inherent, 67
   problem, 11

W

WIN strategy, 153
Wolf, David, 153
word
   giving your, 178
   honoring vs. keeping your, 180
world of humanity, 14
writing, 142

Y

Yalom, Irvin D., 53
You-statements, 88

About the Author

My journey to genuine living began in my twenties when a series of chronic, undiagnosed health problems sidelined the very successful life and career I had enjoyed, leaving me extremely ill, isolated, and unhappy for nearly a decade.

Prior to that, I was the recipient of the prestigious C.D. Howe Memorial Foundation Engineering Award from the Association of Universities and Colleges of Canada and held a President's Citation at the University of Alberta, where I graduated with distinction in Computer Engineering. I have also had the good fortune to work for unique and successful startup companies such as YottaYotta Inc. and Small Army of Nerds Corp.

To this day, I still love engineering, which has taught me that the most interesting problems are *always* people problems. Naturally, I also love relationships, and after several decades of learning to get *real* in them, I have come to trust in the principles and practices of genuine living to consistently create conscious, authentic relationships. My passion for life, relationships, and problem-solving combine in my coaching work, resulting in a pragmatic, no-nonsense approach that is spiritually-oriented and communication-based.

I am now the founder of Genuine Coaching, where through coaching and training with individuals, couples, and organizations, I help my clients create breakthrough results in their personal performance and relationships. Through their triumphs, I surely benefit as much as they do in experiencing greater happiness, freedom, and fulfillment.

I currently live in Toronto, Canada. You can find out more about me and about Genuine Coaching by visiting my website at www.genuinecoaching.ca. I can also be reached by email at info@genuinecoaching.ca.

www.ingramcontent.com/pod-product-compliance
Lightning Source LLC
Chambersburg PA
CBHW070548050426
42450CB00011B/2768